Hound Comics, Inc.
Hound Publishing Division
P.O. Box 803
Levittown, New York 11756

In Jamie's Words... © 2011 Jamie & Anne Isaacs

Publisher's Note
Names, places, characters, events and incidents are products of the
author. All names have been changed to protect the identities of the
persons directly or indirectly involved. The views expressed here
are those of the author and do not necessarily reflect those of Hound
Comics, Inc., Hound Comics, Inc. subsidiaries ...
other organization discussed herein. T
from the personal dairy of the author c
experience.

First Edition

Genre: True-Life / Autobiographical / Historical

ISBN-13: 978-0984695942   ISBN-10: 098469594

PRINTED BY THE TOLEDO GROUP

Foundation for Anti-Bullying, Inc.

Presents

Bullying / Cyber-Bullying
PREVENTION
SUPPORT GROUPS

Ages 12-18

Join 16 year-old Author, Bullying Survivor,
and founder of the
Jamie Isaacs Foundation for Anti-Bullying, Inc.,

Jamie Isaacs

and Anger Management Specialist,
and CEO of **Balance & Power, Inc.**,

Eileen Lichtenstein

For 9 weeks of Bullying Intervention, Anti-Bullying Tactics and Techniques to stay positive and reduce stress and anger. Learn how to stay focused and achieve your goals without obstacles.

Location: To Be Determined
Starting: **Wednesday, June 27th, 2012 7-9 PM**
and continuing for 9 sessions, every Wednesday,
July 11,18,25 & August 1,8,15,22 and 29, 2012

Admission: $5 Donation Per/Child

www.jamieisaacsfoundation**.org**

IN JAMIE'S WORDS

BY JAMIE ISAACS
COWRITTEN WITH ANNE ISAACS

Cover Photography by
Tony Sande/ADA Studios

MY JOURNEY TO FIND PEACE
MY PARENT'S JOURNEY TO
FIND JUSTICE

"IF YOU THINK BULLYING WON'T HAPPEN
TO YOU, YOU'RE WRONG!
IT CAN HAPPEN TO ANYONE,
AT ANY TIME, AT ANY AGE."

ABOUT THE AUTHOR

My name is Jamie Isaacs, I am 15 years old. I live on Long Island, New York with my mom, Anne, my dad, Ron, my brother, Danny, and sister, Lindsey. I attend the Knox School in St. James, where I am getting an amazing education! I love to sing, act, draw, horseback ride, play with my ferrets, read, write and hang out with my friends and family. I am blessed for having so many positive people around me. I love to laugh and am a very happy person. My personality and my upbringing are what saved me.

CONTENTS

ACKNOWLEDGMENTS

A WORD FROM RON ISAACS

ACKNOWLEDGMENTS

I would like to acknowledge the following people:

My Mom and Dad: Thank you for all of your love and support. Because of you, I was able to get through everything! Thank you for always being there for me and helping me express myself in this amazing story!

My brother Danny and sister Lindsey: Thank you for always being there for me.

All of my close friends that I had to leave behind when I changed schools: You are always in my thoughts and we will always remain friends.

The Knox Staff: Thank you for giving me the opportunity of a lifetime at the Knox School, the greatest school I could have ever attended! Thank you so much, I LOVE IT!

All my new friends at Knox: Tommy, Ana, McKenzie, Matt T., Olgies, Nikki, Cici, Annie, Niran, Erik, Bella, Victoria, Dylan, Rachel S., Nate, Thomas, Kat, Emily, Derek, Ryan, Rae, Nadine and Andrey and so many others! Thanks for being so welcoming! YOU'RE AWESOME!!!!

My best friend Isabelle: I haven't known you for very long, but I feel like I've known you my entire life. Nobody quite understands me like you do and I don't know what I would ever do without you in my life. We've been through thick and thin, but that only goes to show the strength we have in our relationship. Nothing can rip us apart. You've always had my back and I will always have yours.

Mrs. White: Thank you for being so welcoming at Knox and for giving me the opportunity to help with the stage direction of the fall play!

Mr. Vibert: Thank you for always believing in my writing and encouraging me to write about my experiences.

Dave at the Teen Center: Thank you for listening to what I had to say at such a young age and for being so kind. You gave me the tactics to stand strong! Thank you for believing me and for helping me through such difficult times. For this I am forever grateful!

A special thanks to Mr. Lartey, for lending an ear to my needs: Thank you for all of the tiresome phone calls you made to the principal and to district office. Thank you for the great advice you gave to my parents and for dealing with my bullying situation with such concern and professionalism! You are a wonderful person and will be blessed for all of your efforts!

Legislator Jon Cooper: Thank you for believing in me and having me assist you in writing the Suffolk County Cyber-bullying Law as well as The School Accountability Law. Thank you for fighting for all of the bullied victims out there. You truly are a hero!

Legislator John Kennedy: Thank you for doing everything possible to keep me and my family safe and protected and for awarding me with a Proclamation for my good deeds. Thank you for always being there to listen.

Mr. Stuart Guthrie: Thank you for taking a personal interest in my writing and for helping me through the creative process.

My Grandmother: Thank you for your constant love and support.
My Grandfather in Heaven: Thank you for giving me the strength to go on. I know you are watching over us and guiding us in the right direction. You will always be in my heart.

A special thank you to Debbie and Erica from The Eventide group for your continued support.

ADDITIONAL ACKNOWLEDGMENTS

TO SENATOR JEFF KLEIN: I would just like to say that it has been an honor to have met you and work with you to help change the world. I look forward to all of the opportunities that you have offered me on this journey. Your heart has been in the right place from the beginning and I commend you for your dedication and undying love for our country. I will stand by your side with great pride for the passing of The New York State Cyber-Bullying Law and hope that this brings a much needed change in our society. I am looking forward to working with you and your staff on other much needed laws that will continue to make our lives and the lives of others better and safer.

TO MAYOR ANDREW HARDWICK: Thank you for all of your support. You are a kind and genuine man and the town of Freeport is lucky to have you as its Mayor. I look forward to continuing the awareness with you and making our neighborhoods a wonderful place to be.

TO BEVERLY FORTUNE: Thank you for making me a part of the Fortune 52 events. I am proud to be a Fortune 52 honoree and look forward to all of the great opportunities that it has to offer. I would just like to say that you are a wonderful person with an extremely big heart and are always looking for other ways to spread love and kindness in our world today. It is a privilege and an honor to know you.

-A Word from Ron Isaacs-

In my own words, it would be difficult to describe what my daughter and my family have been through over the past eight years. I find it difficult to put certain things into words on paper; certain things that have occurred; certain things that have profoundly changed the lives of all of my family members; certain things that have made us all view the world differently; certain things that have made us as a family look at people differently. All of these things are hard, for me anyway, to put into words.

But for my daughter Jamie and my wife Anne, it was a task that had to be done. It had to be done because of what we, as a family, and Jamie, as a human being, have had to endure at the hands of others. Some of these people are selfish and uncaring. Some are downright mean and hurtful. Some of them just didn't want to do their jobs and as a result indirectly caused the spread of a cancer in our school district, a cancer that could have been cured early on in its growth. It had to be done because Jamie and my wife, Anne, wanted others to know our story, in the hope that it may be read by some who may be going through the same thing. Perhaps it will be read by some parents who are going through a similar situation and don't realize what it may be doing to their family.

This book is a true story of bullying and the consequences of not trying to prevent it. It is a story of a little girl, her family, and a school district that just didn't care. A school district that didn't take the measures to ensure that one of its students was safe and was able to learn in an environment that was conducive to learning. It is a story of how two parents went to any length to insure that their child was safe. It is a story about a school district that would do anything to make it look good, after breaking all the basic rules of educational law.

Our story, Jamie's story, had to be told. I know that Jamie hopes that other kids who are being bullied, along with their families, will read this story and that by doing so a life may be saved. Maybe some lonely souls who don't know where to turn for help will read this and find the strength to continue on. Maybe their families will understand what they are going through. This book is not just a story, but a journey through every emotion that a human being can feel, as well as some that are just indescribable.

They say that what doesn't kill you makes you stronger. I can tell you that this experience has strengthened everyone in my family. It has strengthened our convictions, our love, our faith, and our knowing that even though there are people in this world who do bad things, good always prevails over evil.

I am so proud of Jamie for the beautiful young woman that she has become. I am so proud of my wife for the unending dedication to our family and her tireless fight to make things right. I am proud of my family as a whole, for staying strong together, loving each other, and being there for each other, no matter what.

What doesn't kill you makes you stronger! Jamie is alive.

She is a proud survivor.   We are all survivors.

In Jamie's Words

By Jamie Isaacs

Cowritten by Anne Isaacs

This book is dedicated to all the teens that

have taken their lives due to bullying.

You did not die in vain.

I will make sure that your legacy lives on

through the awareness I spread and the laws I

help pass.

INTRODUCTION

It's hard to believe that so much has happened to me. It's almost as if I awoke from a bad dream. If someone would have told me that after 6 long years of bullying and torment, I would have written a book and helped other victims with similar situations in crisis through my foundation, I would have said NEVER! Who would have thought I would be able to overcome such a traumatic time in my life and be able to talk about it freely to schools, camps, library's and political events as if it never happened. This just goes to show you that you can overcome any obstacle that life throws in front of you as long as you willingly accept it and have the strength and determination to fix it.

In Jamie's Words

CHAPTER ONE

THE BEGINNING

I can honestly say that I don't think there will ever be a cure for this infectious epidemic. All the symptoms of this illness will forever be engraved in the back of my mind, like a scar, to continuously remind me of those who hacked away at my innocent childhood, as if it were a block of melting ice. I hope to eventually foresee a bright and happy future, where I can escape this hellhole and am able to live peacefully in a brighter and safer place.

In Jamie's Words

Unfortunately, for those times when I reflect back on my gloomy elementary school years, all there is for me to see are the twisted memories caused by the miserable brats who lived in my neighborhood, those who were too blinded by jealousy to see that I was not the way they thought of me.

I find it incredibly hard to believe that I had only been eight years old when all the bullying started. I also cannot believe that the girl who started it, Amelia, had been my best friend. What is even *harder* to believe is that the principal of the elementary school refused to take any form of action to end this torment being thrust into my life at such a young age. She had the power to end this the moment the situation had been brought to the table. We had full proof of everything that Amelia began to stir up: every incident, every date, every time…everything to prove that this was not just "kids being kids". It *kills* me to know how she neglected to help me and it *kills* me to know that she is still of high authority in the educational system.

In Jamie's Words

Did the principal, *let alone the district,* ever come to the obvious realization that the bullying had a massive impact on my life as well as my whole family? The answer is a straightforward NO. She was too busy running her backwards PTA and failing at attempts to make her hair look like Pete Rose's. As far as the rest of her time went, she was too busy trying to convince the rest of the community that she was a good principal…a good principal who cared about her students. But all of that was just a constantly sugarcoated lie.

I was completely aware of the fact that I was not the only child being bullied in this "breeding ground for bullies". I knew that there were others in the same boat as I was, identical to my situation. The incidents were pushed under the carpet like little grains of dust. At one point, my younger brother, Danny, had even been dragged into this God-forsaken war and was being harassed by the same kids who tormented me, and on occasion, kids who were his own age. Watching Danny being pushed around like a punching bag, without anyone coming to his aid, amazed me, but not in a good way. It

In Jamie's Words

amazed me because, once again, a member of the Isaacs family was being neglected by the school district.

Being so young and naïve meant that it was ten times harder for me to comprehend what was happening to me, my brother, as well as my parents. I was always very open with them and never hid any information from them about what the school was allowing to take place every day. It must have been truly haunting for them to experience such turmoil in their lives, as well as mine. As a parent, you expect to be able to put your child on that big yellow bus and believe your child is going to have a great day at school. You expect her to come home and tell you about all the fun things she did and all the interesting things she learned. Instead, my parents heard about who wouldn't let me play with them, who tripped me on the bus, and who called me a mean and degrading name. You're not even supposed to know what drama feels like until you hit middle school, but not in my case. Every day was just another rerun of the day before. Drama, fear, torture, drama, rumors, more drama, etc…it was a never-ending cycle of neglect and immaturity.

In Jamie's Words

I just wanted to go to school and learn something, because unlike most kids, I enjoyed the idea of school. But I couldn't absorb anything because of the constant distractions from the relentless bullies. I was in a public school, which meant my parents had to pay taxes for me to earn an "education" and those taxes would go to pay the teachers' salaries. What my parents were *really* paying for was disregard and carelessness. I couldn't just get the education and attention I needed as a student. It wasn't fair! Other kids got their education! Some kids were put into a special group in school called *G.A.T.E.* This stands for Gifted and Talented Education, something that I never got a fair chance to be in because of all of the distractions. I definitely could have been in *G.A.T.E.* because I was always very smart and didn't have to study too hard to pass a test. I always paid attention in class and was very diligent with note taking, but when the bullying started, I had problems focusing. That's when things really started to crumble. I started to fail math and spelling; I would get the easiest words and equations wrong. When I was entering 7th grade, I was still struggling in math. If only I had been

In Jamie's Words

able to focus and put my best efforts into my education, I would probably have been in math enrichment instead of remedial math.

I know it's hard to believe that I was still struggling with some aspects of my education, but I would eventually overcome these deficiencies. I have an amazing support system at home; my home life is filled with lots of love, respect, understanding, and fun times. My family and I are a team, which is extremely important in life, not just to overcome bullying, but to overcome any obstacles life might put in front of you. This wonderful support system is what started all of the bullying in the first place. These girls were so jealous of me and my life that they didn't know what to do with themselves but to waste their energy on ruining everything I cherished about life! What they failed to realize is that the bullying and threatening only strengthened my support system. I never felt more love and understanding than I did when I was going through all of this. I always knew that my mom and dad loved me very much, but to see my parents go to such great lengths to protect me was really incredible; my mom wasn't going down without a fight.

In Jamie's Words

We would always say that one day my principal would meet her match…little did we know that she already did: ___MY MOM!___

The whole situation was pretty amusing to see. One by one, parents would start to turn their backs on us, like we were murderers or something. When my mom or dad would come up to the school to pick me and my brother up, we would see parents stare us down and then talk about us as if we weren't even there! That's because the principal wasn't protecting me or punishing the girls who were bothering me; so it gave people a lot to talk about. Maybe they thought that we were making all of the stories up? Why else wouldn't the principal punish the bullies? Maybe that's why everyone turned their backs on us, even some of our closest friends. Maybe they thought that I was the bully. Anything is possible, right? I guess if you really think about it, you would start to question the validity of it too…until it happens to you.

CHAPTER TWO

2nd Grade: WHEN THE CLOUDS ROLL IN

I was overwhelmed with excitement on the first day of second grade. Who wouldn't be? I was only seven, had plenty of friends, and was happy that my brother Danny would be coming to school with me too. After all, I was his older sister; I would be the one to make sure he got to his classroom safely. Even though Danny was only five, he was taller than me, so much taller that his friends would call him "Big D" and he loved it! I was very protective over him, and in return he was the same way to me. Even though he was in kindergarten, we would still sit together on the bus and talk about our day until we got home.

We didn't care about what other people thought about the two of us wanting to stay together. It was wonderful, so I thought. Why wouldn't it be? Second grade is supposed to be this fun! I had everything that I could have ever wanted: My school was only a few minutes away, I had lots of friends, my brother was in school with me, and my mom was always up at the school helping in the classroom for events that we were having (even when she was pregnant with my little sister). Honestly, in my eyes, what could have been better? I guess what I didn't realize was that our lives were about to make a complete 180° turn for the worst. It wouldn't be long before my *best* friend became my *worst* enemy.

Every time Amelia would come over my house, which was often, she had a snide remark about my clothes, my house, etc. At eight years old I didn't realize that she was jealous of my whole entire life. I was too innocent to realize that someone would go out

In Jamie's Words

of her way to try to *destroy* my family and me. At the time, my parents and her parents were fairly close. I thought because of the friendship, that my parents would be able to make some of the nonsense stop. My mom didn't say anything to her mom right away, hoping that the situation would resolve itself. I couldn't blame her for wanting to let things go, because she felt that she had a good relationship with the mom. But, all I could think about was the fact that I was being harassed by one of my best friends. My happiness and security in life was being taken over by frustration and fear due to the fact that this harassment got so bad that Amelia told us that she was going to kill us so that she could live in our house!

It soon began to escalate. Amelia would trip me when I got on the bus, pull out my hair ties, and then proceed to smack me in the face with her backpack. To my dismay, I would get off the bus a complete mess from head to toe; my hair was knotted, my face was scratched, my knees were burned from falling on the rough floor of the bus…and I had witnesses, but none of them came to my defense. My mom wasn't only upset for me, but in a way she was thinking that maybe this was Amelia's Tourette's Syndrome acting out. My mom tried to proceed with caution and discuss this with her mom to see if the Tourette's had been worse the week that a lot of the bullying had gone on. But her mother only contributed to the problem. My mom felt as though she wasn't getting anywhere with the parent, so she decided to go and speak with the principal to see if they could remedy this together. The principal really didn't seem concerned in any way, shape, or form. She told my mom that what happens on the bus isn't her business. In other words, she was claiming that the bus problem was out of her jurisdiction and she wasn't willing to stick her neck out.

It was the second week in April, and we were preparing for my Communion. Unfortunately, I was going to the same church for religion as Amelia. This particular day the religion teacher was out sick so we had to join with another class, Amelia's class. As soon as I walked in she came over to me and **punched** me in the chest. My mom had already left and I went over to the teacher and told her what happened. She really didn't do much either. She told me to sit away from the bully and try not to get upset about it. As soon as religion was over, my mom came to get me and I told her what happened. She took me into the main office and we waited for the director to come in. My mom explained what happened and told her that she must keep her eyes open to this kind of conduct. Luckily, the director apologized and assured us that this wouldn't happen again.

I received communion on April 21st 2004 and happily have not returned to that church! This was upsetting for my mom, since she is from a religious Catholic home. She went to Catholic elementary school, as well as Catholic high school, so why shouldn't she be able to send me to religious instruction without turmoil? My dad, on the other hand, was raised in a Kosher Jewish home. He didn't care that I wanted to receive Communion, because in my home, we shared everything. We were being raised Catholic but we celebrated all the Jewish holidays. My dad wasn't Kosher anymore, since he met my mom and tasted her meatballs, which have lots of cheese in them (when you're Kosher, it is believed that if you eat meat and cheese together, it is a sin).

Well, we were past Communion, but we were still dealing with the bus issues and they were getting worse as the year progressed. You see, some of Amelia's friends were at my Communion party, so it must have irritated her to know how much fun it was without her. I didn't want to go on the bus anymore, but I also didn't want to give in to her; I didn't want her to think that I was backing down and letting her win this battle. But Amelia just continued to harass me on the bus, tripping me, hitting me; you get the idea. So, once again, my mom went up to school several more times to discuss this situation with the principal, but we still got nowhere. My mom then decided to call the bus company and report the mile long list of situations.

Next, my mom went to the district office to speak to the superintendent and he assured my mom that something would be done to rectify this situation. I had to stay on the bus a little longer as we waited to see how the situation would be handled. But, much

In Jamie's Words

to our dismay, nothing was done about it. Finally, my mom went up to school and met with the principal again, who now decided to take **ME** off the bus instead of the bully. This meant that we also had to take my brother off the bus. This wasn't the most convenient situation for my mom, because my dad was working at the deli and my little sister was only turning two. Every day, no matter what the weather conditions were, my mom had to go to the school and wait at the flagpole until my brother and I were released from that prison.

My mom and dad were *really* losing their patience, not only with the principal and superintendent, but also with Amelia's family. So, my mom called Amelia's mom again to try to discuss this situation with her. Needless to say, that conversation didn't go very well. My mom is very diplomatic; she has this gift of being able to talk to people in a very respectful, but direct manner that gets right to the point without insulting the person. After speaking with this ___vulgar___ and ___disrespectful___ parent, my family and I realized where Amelia gets her behavior problems from; you know what they say: *Apples don't fall far from the tree!*

In Jamie's Words

It's sad, don't you think, to be a parent who thinks her child can do no wrong? I mean, nobody's perfect, but to be *that* oblivious? Why couldn't she admit that her child was wrong? Talk about bad parenting…and there were certainly enough witnesses to prove her wrong. I'm sure that some of these witnesses had spoken to her or her **_miserable clone_** of a daughter! Isn't it terrible not being able to say you're sorry? To go through life thinking that you've done nothing wrong? I mean, what's life really about? We're only human, but it takes a big person to say they're sorry. My mom always says *"if you can never admit that you are wrong, then you will never grow to be all that you can be."* It doesn't make you a bad person to have done some bad things; if you are willing to recognize your faults and admit your guilt then it makes up for most of the wrong that you have done. You just have to figure out how to make things right.

I pity this girl and her tribe of friends that found what she did to me the slightest bit amusing. I also pity that disgraceful principal; I mean, really, what kind of an example did this unprofessional

In Jamie's Words

person think that she was setting? How could she look me in the eyes everyday and know that she allowed this immature girl to harass me? Well, the end of the second grade year couldn't come fast enough! With only about four weeks left and me not on the bus anymore...would you believe that the bullying still continued in the school? This despicable child decided to recruit some of the weaker minds to assist in her bullying schemes. One girl she nabbed was a very good friend of mine...or at least I thought she was. So much for thinking that Carol was a close friend, considering she found these schemes to be quite entertaining. Soon, another weak mind was nabbed to assist, my so-called "friend" Mary Jo. Now there were three. Did the principal think that that was cool? Let's face it, three kids bullying me for absolutely no reason is unacceptable and *not* a fun time, whatsoever. These girls got off on the fact that they could follow me around the hall and hiss at me, like they were cats. The best was when they started to stab me with sharpened pencils whenever they got the chance. I would repeatedly go to the nurse's office with puncture wounds in my arms from all of the pencil stabbings, yet the principal did nothing to stop the violence brewing in her school. I would go home and show my parents the wounds and my parents would immediately call the principal to discuss this abuse with her, which got us absolutely nowhere. The only remark the principal gave us, was that I stabbed myself with the pencils! Yeah, right! In my spare time! Because I'm *definitely* the kind of child who would take the pleasure in hurting myself…not!

Soon, Betty joined in and became girl number four. She was my friend also; see the trend? Betty had been best friends with Amelia for years and still is. That's because their two faced parents are friends as well. God! Would I ever catch a break? I just wished this was all over. Why did these rotten girls need to pick on me of all people? I would never wish bullying upon anyone, especially after all of this. And now, there were four and it was getting worse. Finally, after several conversations with the principal, several pencil punctures and bruises due to the **abusive** behavior, plus, several visits from my parents to the principal's office the principal decided to have the four girls and me sit down in her office for mediation.

In Jamie's Words

My mom and I were very excited about this mediation because we actually thought that we were going to make some good headway with this bullying problem. Boy, were we wrong! The principal called everyone into her office and asked me and the other girls what was going on; she basically asked us to hash it out! All of the girls involved denied doing anything. Amelia claimed that she never bothered me and that she wanted to be my friend! What a load of crap. Carol said that I was the one doing all of the bullying and that she didn't want to be my friend anymore! Mary Jo said that my mom did all of my homework for me while I sat around and did nothing! Betty said that I was the one causing all of the problems! So, I got really upset and started to cry. At eight years old, you really don't know what else to do. I couldn't believe that they would all lie to the principal and hurt me like that. I was always such a good friend to all of them and this is what I got in return.

Then, Mary Jo said she was sorry! She admitted to harassing me and hissing at me because she was told to do so by Amelia. She also admitted to making up the story about my mom doing all of my homework. Admitting this in front of these girls and the principal should have been an eye opening experience, but it wasn't. Don't you think at that point the **stupid** principal would have realized that the other girls were lying and would have given them some sort of punishment? NO, that would've been the NORMAL thing to do! Remember, this principal is anything but NORMAL! The principal only wanted us to mend the fence and move on with our "merry" ways.

That evening we were all really upset and agitated at what happened with the mediation. My mom decided to call Carol's mom and discuss with her what took place in the principal's office. Carol's mom said that she didn't think it was nice what her daughter had said to me and that she would talk to her. I was relieved that we had finally gotten somewhere with one of the bullies' parents, but that didn't mean that I was going to forgive her. The next day I was filled with lots of anxiety; I didn't want to go to school because I was totally sick to my stomach. My mom kept me home that day and notified the principal as to why I wouldn't be there.

In Jamie's Words

As far as the conversation that my mom had with the other parent, it obviously did nothing, because when I returned to school, nothing had changed. If anything, the girls were all laughing at me because they all thought it was funny how they had gotten over on the principal. These stupid girls think they got away with something really funny. How would they like it if the tables were turned and they were getting the brunt of the abuse? Or how about the idiotic principal; did she find humor in my sadness too? All I could think about was going home to be with my family; I couldn't think about school or studying. All I could think about was how stressed out I was and how I didn't want to go to school anymore and deal with these miserable people. My mom was absolutely furious that this was never ending. She went back to the principal's office and again explained how disappointed she was in the way she was handling the situation. She told her that because of her and the way she handled things, I couldn't focus or pass a simple test. My mom went on to tell her that we were going to have to hire a tutor to help me pass my tests, due to what was happening. My mom stormed into the superintendent's office and discussed this matter with him too. Well, as always, he had no idea that the principal had a powwow with me and these girls, so he had to contact her to get the whole pathetic story! He proceeded to tell my mom that after he got the whole story, he would contact us to discuss the alternatives. Yeah right! Alternatives, what alternatives? Punishing these disgusting girls, calling their parents, and making it right for me had clearly been left out of their discipline book.

The amazing part is that my dad had a prior relationship with this superintendent. My dad had major spine surgery due to an accident and the superintendent had spine problems as well and was using the same surgeon's office. So, periodically, my dad would see him in this doctor's office and just talk about whatever was going on. Mostly, the discussions were about the superintendent's family and kids and how important they were to him. Wow, was he the only one in the world with kids… or shall I say: important kids? What about me and my brother and sister? Were we invisible? Maybe to him we were!

In Jamie's Words

Needless to say, the superintendent never got back to us regarding my horrendous situation and the end of the year was quickly approaching. Maybe he was too busy visiting one of his kids at college? As a second grader, you wouldn't expect me to understand the corruptness in the school system, but I happened to be extremely mature for my age and was able to understand what the school was allowing to happen to me. Even though I had the support of my parents, I still found myself crying all the time and making myself throw up so I didn't have to go to school. I wound up forcing myself to go anyway, just so that I wouldn't feel as though the bullies had gotten the best of me.

When I *did* go to school, I started to make myself feel sick so that I could go to the nurse's office and possibly go home. On the average, I probably went to the nurse 3-4 times a week toward the end of the year. At times, the nurse seemed to be completely beside herself. She couldn't believe that I was so sick to my stomach that I had to go home early a few times a week and nothing was being done about it by the principal or her staff. The principal didn't have any kids, so what did she know about raising a family? Let's face it, how could she give advice or have the compassion for a child in need if she herself had never experienced it first hand?

All I could think about was how cruel she was to me and my family. I decided, with my parents, that I wanted to move; I wanted to move out of the district. I remember back five years ago at the pain my mom was feeling. Don't forget that I not only lost my friends, but so did my mom. These girls who were bullying me were my friends, and their parents were very friendly with mine. They used to come over all the time and hang out with us, but that obviously changed. So this whole situation really took its toll on the whole family. We were all suffering.

I remember my mom going back up to the school at the end of the year to pick me up early, because I was at the nurse's office again. This time, it was because I started to hit myself in the mouth with my water bottle. Of course it was bad, but it was better than wanting to kill myself. I hit myself so hard repeatedly, that I gave myself a purple bruise above my lip and I wouldn't stop until my lip

In Jamie's Words

was swollen and some of the skin was worn away. It sounds ridiculous, doesn't it? That I would intentionally hurt myself? Well, at the time it didn't seem so ridiculous. My body was filled with so much anxiety; I didn't know what to do. My brain was bursting with questions I wanted answered, but no one was there to listen. I had so much anger inside of me. I loathed these girls and that school, and that principal! I guess hitting myself seemed like the only alternative to getting my point across to the school. I don't know who really noticed except maybe the nurse. But all she really did for me was give me ice to help with the swelling.

Now that's not *exactly* what I wanted, but I did get *someone's* attention. My mom was always so beside herself when she would come to pick me up and see me disheveled. You could see the pain written all over her face, as if it was written in a thick black Sharpie Marker. I didn't know what hurt me more, the bruise on my lip or the pain in my heart for my mother. The nurse would always step outside of her office to talk to my mom and it was obvious that the nurse was just as distraught. The nurse was really

In Jamie's Words

sweet for actually caring about me, unlike everyone else in that hell hole. She would always make me feel like it was going to be okay even though I knew it wasn't true; she had this calming concerned way about her. Honestly, at that time, she was the only school employee that really cared.

After speaking with the nurse, my mom got my things together and as we started to leave, we saw my 2nd grade teacher, Mrs. Peters, coming down the hall. My mom stopped and waited. Mrs. Peters was devastated when she saw me. She rushed to my side and wrapped her arms around me. Just like everyone else, she told me that everything was going to be okay. Only this time, it *was* going to be okay, because the year was just about over. When we got home, my mom took pictures of my lip and then immediately dropped them off for developing, to save as proof that I was under lots of stress from what was going on in school. She also called the doctor and made an appointment for me to be seen as soon as possible; in the event I had done serious damage to the skin.

49

In Jamie's Words

Surprisingly, I went to school the next day, but I wasn't happy. While I was in school, praying that I would just have a normal day, my mom once again went to the district office to see the superintendent, Mr. Buckley. This time, she had the pictures of my lip with her. Mr. Buckley urgently took my mom into his office. She showed him the photos and expressed her concern for my safety and well being; nothing she hadn't done before. Once again, the superintendent promised to get to the bottom of this. He gave us his word that he would talk to the principal and make things right for me; just another empty promise. Before I knew it, the end of the year was here. It was the last day of school and still no phone call from Mr. Buckley. Nothing was done to these girls. They basically had a field day with me and my emotions. Then again, so did the principal and the superintendent. My mom was very annoyed, to say the least, and so was I. She couldn't believe that no one took a stand for me or for what was right...well, actually, she could believe it; what she couldn't believe was how careless a school district could be.

In Jamie's Words

Lots of people had judgmental remarks behind our backs, but no one did anything to help us; not even parents who had witnessed all of this happening. Some parents expressed their condolences to my mom, like I was dead! I pity all of these people that were too shallow to come to my aid and my parents' aid in our time of need. Did they think that something like this would never happen to them? Did they think that bullying was nonexistent in their children's worlds? They were all too self-absorbed and too concerned with ridiculing me and my family.

My mom was taking this really bad, to say the least. It made my mom think back to her childhood when she was adopted at birth and raised by a very loving mother and father. All she kept saying was "why?" How could she raise me with such love and then see me get so much hate in return? We were such a caring and generous family. Could this have been the driving force that led to my betrayal? My mom told me that when she was younger she had always struggled with rejection because she was adopted and now she was viewing this as another form of rejection. Why weren't these kids accepting me? She couldn't understand. My dad wasn't too happy either. Even though he was raised by a religious Jewish family, there was still so much pain in his household. His mom had left when he was only 11 and his dad worked three jobs to support him and his sister. When his dad came home, if all the chores weren't done, my dad would get a beating. This behavior that was being cast upon me infuriated him. He had lived with so much pain his whole life until he met my mom and fell in love, with not only her, but her family. Our home life was so perfect. We were all so loving toward one another. My dad promised himself that he would never lay a hand on any of his children the way his mother and father did to him and now, right before his eyes, these kids were destroying me and he couldn't stop it.

CHAPTER THREE

3rd GRADE "Wilting"

The summer had been short, but filled with lots of love and fun times with my parents. My parents got me a tutor over the summer to help with math and spelling. I guess they figured that this would stop me from falling behind. So, once a week my mom would take me to the library for an hour and I continued with this tutor for about six months. My parents also signed me up for acting classes at a well known acting school. The acting school did a lot of fun

In Jamie's Words

exercises with us; it helped me to come out of my shell and definitely helped with my social skills. Within just a few weeks, I gained a lot of my self esteem back. I made some friends and they helped me to get my mind off of things.

Summer was ending and even though I was still going to acting classes, I was nervous about going back to school. About two weeks before school started, Amelia, who lived about 2 blocks away from me, started to ride her bike past my house all the time. Sometimes she would purposely stop at my mailbox and wait for a few seconds. Whenever one of my parents saw her, they would immediately go outside and tell her to get away from our property. Can you imagine the nerve of this kid? Don't tell me she had nothing else better to do. Where were her parents? Didn't they care about how far she was riding her bike? I guess not. It was almost as if they were raising her like an animal. Maybe she felt inner strength because the principal would give her positive reinforcement for negative behavior; therefore she had grown to be a disgusting monster.

In Jamie's Words

My mom and dad did some research and looked into sending me for counseling free of charge, so they left several messages with a local teen center. While waiting for the teen center to return our calls, we had other things to worry about. With school just around the corner, I needed to be mentally ready to begin. My parents told me repeatedly that if they had to, they would also consult with an attorney to see what we could do legally about these girls, their families, and the school.

I felt pretty good about the whole attorney thing; there would finally be someone willing to help me. My mom and dad knew several attorneys, so I figured that it would be pretty easy for them to consult with one. I wasn't going to be consumed with the attorney thing; that would be something my parents would take care of and then just fill me in. The first day of school came before I was ready. I was excited to see my friends, but wasn't excited to see the bullies. The interesting thing was that over the summer, I was invited to a birthday party and Carol was there. She kept trying to talk to me, like everything was just fine and dandy between us. I just wanted to

In Jamie's Words

be left alone, but my mom told me to give her a chance and that maybe she would apologize. So, I gave her a chance and she did say she was sorry for hurting my feelings in school and for listening to the bully. So, I did what any other eight year old kid would do: I tried to forgive her and just move on as if nothing had happened. The first day of school was here and I met Carol in front so we could walk to class together; everything seemed really good. I walked into my third grade class with confidence, knowing that this would be a new year with new friends and a new teacher. My teacher, Mrs. Hemmingway, seemed, nice. So, I hoped for the best.

The next day, September 8th, 2005 wasn't so great. My mom dropped my brother and me off at school and as soon as my brother was out of my sight, the infamous Amelia was right behind me. I heard her loud and clear saying degrading things to me, but I didn't turn around. I just kept walking down to my classroom with my heart racing. I felt better, or shall I say, safer, once I got to my classroom. After lunch, we had recess. I didn't really enjoy playing on the playground because the sand was filled with broken glass and cigarette butts. So, I would sit under a shady tree and write, minding my own business.

When recess was over, we all went back inside the classroom. That's when my friend Halley came over to me frantically saying, "Amelia came over to me on the playground and told me to hurt you. And if I didn't, she was going to hurt *me!*" Later that day, Halley and I went to Mrs. Hemmingway and told her what had happened with the new threat that Amelia had made. She asked us to go to the principal and discuss it with her and that she would discuss this with her as well. Sadly, the principal still did nothing to Amelia about this threat. I suppose Amelia had now found a new hobby to add onto her old hobby of torturing me- threatening other kids to hurt me. Maybe to her it's not so wrong. Once again, my mom was back at the superintendent's office; she was becoming a well known face there. I was starting to think that they were going to give her an office there. The superintendent told my mom that he would put a stop to this and speak to the principal and that he would make sure that something was done immediately to stop this

In Jamie's Words

bullying. I think the only thing that he did right away was to tell his staff not to allow any more calls through to his office if they were regarding me. Basically, we were once again at the mercy of the principal and the district and they were doing nothing to protect me from this evil.

My mom sent in a note to Mrs. Hemmingway regarding these issues so that maybe we could set up a conference. After reading the note, Mrs. Hemmingway called my mom and told her that she could come in to speak to her. When my mom sat down with her, she said that she couldn't understand why nothing was being done to protect me. Once again, we had a witness who told the principal the story and yet no punishment was ever given. She went on to tell my mom what a good kid I was and that I didn't deserve this cruelty from the kids or the district. Mrs. Hemmingway went on to say that she would do her best to shield me from these girls. That was well and good, but what about the principal and the superintendent?

In Jamie's Words

My parents were growing desperate. They went down to the local police department to try to make a claim against the school and the girls individually. But to our dismay, the police said that the girls were minors and that we needed to go after the school legally. With that, my mom called several attorneys and went through the whole story with them, only to have them say that we still needed more evidence. Was being emotionally and physically abused not enough? What was this world coming to? A child can't even go to school to get an education? Didn't anyone in that district read between the lines? Didn't they see that eventually more things were going to happen and that it would only escalate from here? Obviously not!

Well, the weeks to come were no better. More and more people were hearing about what was happening from the bullies' parents. Little by little, parents started to ostracize my mom, and little by little kids were shying away from me. I guess that it was easier to befriend the bully than to stay friends with me. I once heard a parent tell her child not to be friends with me anymore because if they stayed friends with me then they would get bullied too. The sad thing was that this girl was one of my closest friends; her name was Sabrina. I loved hanging out with her and but as the new routine goes, that all changed. What kind of *sick, twisted* people are there in this world? Did they think that saying that would protect their child? Why didn't my friends parents come to my aid? My mom would have done that for their kids. No one came to my aid except my mom and dad. They were there for me through it all. I would discuss it with my grandparents, but not too often, because my grandfather wasn't well and I didn't want to upset him.

Anyway, my third grade teacher, Mrs. Hemmingway, did what she could to protect me from these girls, but they had turned into monsters at this point. If you robbed a bank and got away with it and then kept on robbing banks and nothing was ever done to reprimand or punish you, how mentally strong and confident would you have become? It was like they were unstoppable! Can you imagine? A gang of eight year old girls are *unstoppable*? How embarrassing, not just for the school, but for their parents. Did they go home and pretend to have done nothing wrong? If only the principal would have contacted their parents, maybe these girls would have had a different outlook on life. I mean, did the principal think that she was helping these girls? I truly don't know what could have been going through the principal's mind. What happened to **zero tolerance**? I was told by the principal herself that the school didn't tolerate any kind of bullying. So, what happened? All of a sudden did the moronic principal become in favor of it?

As the days went on, the bullying continued. My mom and dad enrolled me in some karate classes to help me with self defense. I liked it for a little while, but it really wasn't my thing. I didn't want to have a fistfight with these girls. I just wanted them to stop bullying me. So eventually I dropped out of karate. I really wanted to just drop out of school, but my parents did everything possible to keep reassuring me that everything would be alright. After a while, the bullying really became ridiculous! I mean how many months was this going to continue? Weren't these girls sick and tired of harassing me? Or was it just starting to get fun for them? These stupid girls were wasting their young lives on harassing me.

In Jamie's Words

Meanwhile, I was the one still sitting under the tree at recess with a bunch of friends that weren't going to tolerate their bullying. I was the one that would draw beautiful pictures in my sketch book at recess and write poems and even songs, while they would stand over me and try to take my friends away. Mrs. Hemmingway would see them come over to me and bother me and she would come over and tell them to leave me alone. Thankfully, she put some effort into helping me.

Finally, we heard from the social worker, Don, and we went to speak to him. We all had a chance to talk to him in detail. I wasn't afraid to tell him what was going on. Actually, I couldn't wait. What a burden I had been carrying on my shoulders for all these months. I felt like a weight had been lifted off of my chest. It was kind of interesting because he was a social worker trained in all aspects of therapy; he had a lot of really great ideas for me as well as for the whole family. The most important thing was that he was going to give us weekly appointments every Thursday evening at 6:00 pm. I was very happy to hear that he was going to see us on a weekly

In Jamie's Words

schedule. It made me feel like he believed me. We would go to Don's office every Thursday for about 1 hour. My family and I really enjoyed it; it was an opportunity to vent to someone who was a stranger to me, and yet someone who I had completely trusted. He would give me some great ideas on how NOT to let these girls bother me or distract me. He would teach me how to stay focused in school while dodging all these bullets (as if we were in combat). He tried to use war as an example of staying focused. He explained that these girls and their families must be very **_SHALLOW_** people. He helped me to turn my tears into laughter at them for being so self absorbed and immature.

As far as my parents went, Don also listened to my mom's pain as a parent watching her child suffer. He would tell my mom every week to not show me how upset or bothered she was about this situation. I actually think that he himself was a little taken back at the fact that the principal wasn't doing anything to stop all of the bullying and threats. My family and I continued weekly visits with

Don until school ended. It was a blessing to have him, because as you can guess, the bullying lasted until the last day of school!

On April 22, 2005, my friend, Halley, came over my house for a play date. A few minutes after we got home, Amelia and her mom pulled up in their car in front of our house. They both got out of the car and proceeded to make a scene on my front lawn yelling and screaming things at our house. My friend and I stood at the door and watched this ridiculous scene. I remember my mom telling us not to open the door and that she was going to call the police. After Halley left, the police came to my house and took a statement. My mom and I told the police officer what happened. After leaving our home, the police officer went to Amelia's house to speak with them regarding the trespassing and harassment. Then the officer came back to our house and told us that he gave them a warning and if they stepped a foot on our property again, they would be arrested. That made me pretty happy.

In Jamie's Words

That evening Halley's mother called the house and spoke with my mom. She told my mother that she was really sorry that I was being bullied and that I had to experience that situation today, but Halley didn't want any part of it and they didn't want her involved with me. Her mom said that she instructed her daughter not to say what happened today to anyone. Amazing, isn't it? Once again, here's another parent who won't stick up for me or my family even when their kid was a witness. But yet, if something happened to their kid, they would want a witness right away. It's very sad. No one was willing to step up to the plate. My family and I were just going to continue to be innocent victims for a crime that would repeatedly happen over and over again for the next few years.

On June 23, 2005, the other third grade classes all got small autograph books from their teachers. Mrs. Hemmingway's class was not included in this. It's unknown why her class was left out. Once again, it was an example of the wonderful school I attended. Anyway, I was hanging out with some of my friends under a tree, drawing, when my other so called friend, Kerry, came over and

In Jamie's Words

asked me to sign her autograph book. I willingly agreed and signed her book. When she walked away I noticed that Amelia was waiting for her. She walked over to Amelia and gave her the autograph book. Then Amelia turned around and looked in my direction and yelled "Thanks Jamie for signing my autograph book!" I couldn't believe that Kerry would do that to me. I felt so betrayed.

When I got home, I told my mom what happened. My mom told me to call Kerry's house and talk to her; so I did. I asked Kerry why she made me think that I was signing her autograph book when the whole time Amelia had put her up to it. She said that she didn't know. I told her that I was really upset at her for doing that to me. I told her that friends don't treat friends that way and that I would never be able to trust her again. After I spoke to her my mom got on the phone with her mom. Her mom, Donna, said that she wanted a few minutes to speak with Kerry to find out why she did what she did and that she would call my mom back. A few minutes later she called back and apologized for her daughter's actions. Then Kerry got on the phone and apologized to me.

In Jamie's Words

My mom and dad wrote a letter to the superintendent, Mr. Buckley, stating what had happened. They were very direct with him and clearly stated that they had retained an attorney and they were getting ready to sue. Upon receipt of the letter, Mr. Buckley's office called our house to set up an appointment to speak with him. The meeting took place approximately one week after receipt of the letter. When my parents arrived, they went into Mr. Buckley's office along with the principal. At this meeting, my parents discussed the issue of my safety and well being at the school. The superintendent requested that we not proceed with any lawsuits yet. He told my parents that he would fix the problem and repeatedly assured them at this meeting that he would take care of this situation. Also, at this meeting, the principal said that she would contact Kerry's parents to confirm the story about the signing of the autograph book. At that point, my mom and dad left. They came home and told me what had happened. A day or two later, the principal called my house and spoke to my mom. She told her that she spoke with Kerry's mother and confirmed that Kerry and Amelia did in fact pull an

In Jamie's Words

underhanded scheme. Her mom went on to tell the principal that her daughter was a victim because she was put up to this scheme. Anyway, the principal said that she spoke with Amelia's mother and told her what her daughter did. Then, the principal assured my mom that she would give a punishment to Amelia when school started back up again. Because as you must have already realized, "SCHOOL'S OUT FOR THE SUMMER!"

CHAPTER FOUR

4th GRADE "Barely Noticed"

Just in case you were wondering about Amelia's punishment from the end of third grade, **IT NEVER HAPPENED**! Not only didn't it happen, but the superintendent, Mr. Buckley--- RETIRED!

Fourth grade was no picnic either. Even though my parents had gone to the principal and the district numerous times, Carol still wound up in my class. The whole idea here was to protect me from these girls so that maybe I could get an education that my parents' tax dollars were paying for. You would think that by now the school would accommodate me just so that they would not have to deal with my angry parents. Not a chance! It was almost as if it was done on purpose. My parents wrote a letter to the 4th grade teacher, Mrs. Smith, explaining the situation. She called us and said that she would keep an eye out. Big deal, keeping an eye out wasn't supposed to be the plan. Being able to focus in class and pass my tests without any distractions was the plan. Well, nevertheless, the principal left us together the whole year in the same class.

Every day I would go to school with a knot in my stomach. Even though Mrs. Smith supposedly kept an eye out, Carol harassed me every single day until the last day of school. Can you imagine if Mrs. Smith didn't keep an eye out? My mom would have to force me to get out of bed and get ready for school. Then she would have to force me to eat. Then she would have to force me to get in the car so that she could drive me to school. It was really getting ridiculous! My parents didn't want to take me out of that school. They wanted me to stick it out until our house was sold and I would switch schools with my brother and little sister. Honestly, how many times does a parent have to go to school and complain to the teacher, the school psychologist, the principal, the assistant principal and the district before something gets done! Just thinking back about everything that happened to me gets me very angry and disappointed!

The interesting thing was that my mom asked my third grade teacher if she could tutor me since she was retiring and she said yes. So, on a weekly basis Mrs. Hemmingway would come to our home and tutor me. Almost every time she would leave our house, Amelia would be near our mailbox or would be riding her bike past my house. Sometimes she would even stop to say hello to Mrs. Hemmingway and other times she would just stop and stare. When my mom would go outside and see her there, she would tell her to leave. Mrs. Hemmingway witnessed this happening all the time. Honestly, for what reason other than to try to know my business, was she stalking me and my family? Here my mom was paying to have me learn what I couldn't learn in school because of her and the

In Jamie's Words

other girls. Now she decides to come to my house and stalk me? My mom had even called the police to say that the girl that was bothering me in school was now stalking me at home and the police said that there was nothing they could do because Amelia and her friends were minors! ***NOTHING THEY COULD DO? WHAT IF THIS WAS THEIR KID? WHAT WOULD THEY DO THEN?***

Anyway, by the time my mom dropped me off at school I was already a bundle of nerves and the day hadn't even begun. Mrs. Smith would do her best to control the situation while I was in her class, but at lunch and recess CHAOS WOULD BREAK LOOSE! At lunch, Carol would get up from her seat and come over to me and stand in front of me and slam her hands down on the table and yell at me. Sometimes I would yell back at her and tell her to leave me alone, and other times I would try to ignore it. Either way it didn't stop. Maybe I should have stood up and hit her. That would've probably gotten me detention and also some satisfaction, but I chose not to be violent. I was alone in this fight while she was one of four bullies that would have probably joined in to hit me back. After lunch, we would have recess which was just as much fun as lunch. I would sit under a tree with a couple of my friends and we would sit and draw or write in our journals. Unfortunately, I guess that bothered Carol also. She would grab Betty and Amelia and have them come over to the tree and harass me. They would stand in front of me and my friends and they would tell my friends not to hang out with me. They said that my friends would have more fun with them. Sometimes one or two of them would get up and leave with them and sometimes we would all stick together and tell them to take a hike and leave us alone. Eventually, I found that the girls they would prey upon were very weak minded girls and if they were willing to get up and hang out with Carol, Betty and Amelia, then they really weren't my friends anyway.

By now, I had started to suffer from anxiety as well as refluxing my food. That means that acid was coming up from my stomach and burning my esophagus and the back of my throat due to stress! Think about it. I couldn't eat in peace so I was rushing and shoving my food down pretty quickly. I couldn't relax under a tree

In Jamie's Words

with my friends because that was bothering them also, so basically

my whole day was filled with non-stop ANXIETY! The crazy part

was that Mrs. Smith had recess duty with our class. But I guess her

eye was too busy to watch and protect me because she would play

kick ball every day at recess. I had even gone over to her several

times to ask her to please speak to Amelia, Carol and Betty and get

them to leave me alone so that I could enjoy my recess. I think that

was probably too much to ask because instead of punishing these

bullies, she took away my recess and had me be a helper in some of

the younger classes. So, what was I supposed to do? She was

basically telling me that she wasn't going to waste her time

protecting me, so she would rather not have to worry about me at all.

That's not fair. Why should I be punished? Did I really have a

choice? If I said no to being a helper, than I was at risk of being

bullied at recess every day. So, having no options, I had to accept

what was dealt to me and every day I gave up my recess and I

helped out in another classroom. Of course, my parents were furious and they went up to school again, and back to the district again but as you already know it got us NOWHERE!

Basically, I guess you can say that 4th grade was pretty bad. Wasn't any teacher going to take a stand for me? My parents went and spoke to the assistant principal, Mr. Meyers, who told them that he knew exactly what was going on and that his hands were tied! **TIED! What does that mean?** You mean to tell me that you're aware of all of the abusive behavior and harassment but you can't do anything to help me because you're told not to help me by the principal? What kind of school was I attending? Was it a school or a **_CIRCUS?_** How could Mr. Myers accept what the principal told him about not helping me? For God's sake, I'm just a kid! Is this some kind of vendetta she had against me and my family? **_What kind of sick principal is she!_** How could someone go out of their way to hurt an innocent child? How could Mr. Myers agree with her decision not to help me? He had kids, how would he feel if this was happening to him and his family? See, that's my point. It wasn't happening to his family, it was happening to mine! Why would the

In Jamie's Words

principal care, she didn't have any kids, so what did she know about caring and loving a child? **NOTHING!**

The interesting thing was that Mr. Myers had a son that worked around the block from my family's deli. Everyday Bill would come in for lunch and discuss the situation with my mom regarding the bullying. This wasn't your everyday disagreement with another student. This bullying situation was out of control. This was and still is probably the worst case of bullying this district has ever seen and allowed! Needless to say, I couldn't wait for the year to end. I was so done with all of the bull. I was losing friends like crazy, my parents were truly beside themselves and the anxiety was just building.

CHAPTER FIVE

5th GRADE "Shattered"

Things started out OK. The class I was in was pretty good. I had heard both good and bad things about the fifth grade teacher, Mr. Dickson. I would still get the occasional stares in the hallway or at recess, but for the time being it seemed calmer. Even though it was better, I never let my guard down. Don't forget that by now the bullying had been going on for a little over two years. My mom and dad were hoping that maybe these girls grew up over the summer.

In Jamie's Words

I joined a few clubs, like CD Yearbook and The Special Olympics. I really enjoyed these clubs. I loved helping the Special Ed kids with their motor skills and preparing them for the Special Olympics Competition. I felt really good about it. It made me really happy to put a smile on their faces.

I had made some new friends, but what I didn't realize was that some of these new friends were friends with the bullies. I didn't want to lose them as friends so I just went with it and hoped for the best. It was going good for a few months. It was probably the longest I had ever gone without a problem since the end of second grade, until Mr. Dickson started to call me names. He thought that he was being funny, but he wasn't. If I wore my winter jacket, which at the time was camouflage, Mr. Dickson would call me "G.I. JANE." If I wore a shirt with glitter or sequins on it, he would call me "BRITNEY SPEARS." Then if I had on a top with a little jacket he would call me "JANET JACKSON." The worst was when I wore shirts with horses on them. Horses are my favorite animal, so I had a few shirts with horse imprints on them. Mr. Dickson would call me

In Jamie's Words

"RAINBOW DONKEY." My parents couldn't believe it at first. But then I brought home "NO HOMEWORK PASSES" with the names "ICE T." and "ICE CUBE" on them.

The next day my mom went to school and spoke to Mr. Dickson and asked him to please stop calling me these names, even if he found them to be amusing. My mom went on to tell him that it was ruining the morale in the class and that I had enough trouble with kids and I didn't need any more. Mr. Dickson didn't seem to care. He said that he would stop, but that it was completely harmless.

Well, he didn't stop, he continued! Now instead of just him calling me names, the class would chime in with him. For instance, one day he called me "RAINBOW DONKEY" and some of the kids started to call me "JACK***." This is exactly what my parents and I were afraid of. I begged Mr. Dickson to please stop calling me names, but he didn't. Instead he would tell the kids in the class to stop calling me names, but he continued.

In Jamie's Words

My parents went down to the district to speak with the new superintendent only to find out that he knew nothing about the bullying situation with me. My mom filled out a harassment complaint form and gave it to the woman at the front desk who supposedly gave it to the school's compliance officer. The compliance officer obviously did nothing with it and as far as going back to the school to discuss it with the principal; I guess that wasn't an option. As you can see by now the principal took me from the frying pan and put me into the FIRE! All I kept thinking was that I would finally have a chance to grow both educationally and mentally. I guess I thought wrong.

By now my parents had had conversations with almost every educational attorney on Long Island and some in Manhattan. Some attorneys told my parents all the laws and rules that were violated, while others said that there wasn't enough yet to sue. To me and my family it didn't matter that these kids were all minors, the teacher wasn't a minor; what about him? My parents were growing more and more upset and stressed out over the situation.

In Jamie's Words

They were banging their heads against the wall trying to get the right attorney to take this case, aside from the stress of having these girls bothering me on a daily basis. The incidents had still been happening on a daily basis with your typical teasing, staring and talking under their breath about me, but the real bullying hadn't started until right before my birthday at the end of March 2006.

I started to chat on AIM a lot. It seemed like a lot of fun. Anyway, one of my other friends, Josephine, started to be mean to me. At first I wasn't sure if it was related to the other girls bothering me or if this was going to be something new. Josephine would come over my house and tell me that if I didn't do what she wanted that she would break all of my special things in my room. Then I got an instant message from her on AIM saying that she was going to break into my house and steal all of our expensive things. I just kept thinking to myself, "Is this a joke? Is this girl serious?" Well, my birthday party was 2 days later so I tried to smooth things over with her for the time being because I didn't need any more problems. I

In Jamie's Words

told her that if she was going to act like that then she couldn't come to my party, nor could we stay friends.

Well, needless to say, she showed up at my house for my party, told me she was sorry and we tried to get along. The truth of the matter was that she really just wanted to come to my birthday party; she really didn't care about mending the fence with me. Right after my party, everything went back to the way it was before with her. Her lousy behavior, her snide remarks, her hanging around with Amelia and Carol; it was getting crazy again and now there were FIVE! It wouldn't be long until more bullies joined the club. It's like I said earlier, if you could rob a bank and get away with it, then, why not rob a bank on a daily basis?

Friday, March 30, 2006 at 2:15 pm., I was on the playground at recess. I was sitting on the parallel bars with some friends when the bullies started to give me dirty looks from the other set of monkey bars. I went to get off the bars and I slipped because there was a sharp ridge in the bars where they were soldered. I spun around the bars, flipped over and then fell to the ground into sand that contained shards of broken glass. I was crying and yelling in pain. I wasn't sure what part of my body I hurt, but I was in a lot of pain. The bullies all gathered around me and started laughing and mimicking me. Mr. Dickson came over to me with the assistant principal who, by the way, also taught 5th grade. Mr. Myers got all the girls away from me while some of my friends ran to the nurse for help. The nurse came out with a wheelchair and I was helped getting into it. I stayed at the nurse's office until my dad came to get me. While my dad was in the nurse's office, the dismissal bell rang. As all the kids started to exit the building, the bullies had recruited another girl named Mary.

Mary and I had been friendly because my brother and her brother were friends and her older brother helped out in my family's deli. While my dad was in the nurse's office, the bullies and Mary walked by and Mary made it a point to put her head into the nurse's office and say "Hey, Jamie are you hurt?" Then they all started to laugh until they realized that my dad was there. My father didn't say anything to them. He just wheeled me to the car and took me home.

In Jamie's Words

My dad took me to the hospital at approximately 5pm. My mom left work early and came straight to me. I was very upset. They had me in a private room because at first they thought that my pelvis was broken. After my mom had gotten there she requested a female doctor to examine me. We had to wait a while before someone got there. When the gynecologist examined me she said that it wasn't a broken pelvis; it was probably just sore. I had a laceration in my private area, something that would compare to an episiotomy. They also examined my foot because it hurt to walk and they saw that my toe was broken. My mom wanted a second opinion because the doctor wanted to give me stitches down there and I was scared, so I had to wait for the night shift to come in to examine me. When the next set of doctors arrived they, too wanted to stitch me. The laceration wasn't very long but it was really deep. I was screaming and very upset and uptight. I didn't want anyone to touch me. The doctor was trying to calm me down, but it wasn't working. She called in another female doctor for her opinion and that doctor

In Jamie's Words

wanted to glue it. I really started to freak out. GLUE IT? I couldn't imagine.

My mom asked the doctors if we could just leave it and put some A&D on it along with soaking the area in a sitz bath. They reluctantly agreed. They told my mom to get a Perry squeeze bottle and fill it with lukewarm water, rinse the area often and then put A&D on at night. They told us that this healing process was going to take a few weeks since I declined the option for stitches or glue. Honestly, I really didn't care how long it took to heal, just as long as I was out of the hospital and home! The next day I was in a lot more pain. I could hardly walk, and I would cry every time I had to go to the bathroom. All I could think about were those horrible girls! How dare they put me in this position! It was the start of spring break and I was bedridden while they were probably enjoying themselves.

That Monday, April 2nd, my mom took me up to school even though they were closed for the break. We spoke to the office manager and the secretary. They wrote everything down and

In Jamie's Words

apologized for the inconvenience. My mom asked if the principal could please contact us to discuss this matter right away. We were told that she was away on an African safari and when she returned, she would call us.

What do you think happened? If you're thinking what I was thinking, "Maybe a tiger swallowed her up, or she developed malaria" you're wrong! If you're guessing that the principal never called, than you're correct! SO MUCH FOR WISHFUL THINKING!

That same day, my dad was at work and he saw the assistant principal's son, Bill. My dad asked him if he would please call his dad and give him our home and cell numbers because it was important that we speak to him right away. After my dad called the house to tell us that he spoke with Bill, Mr. Myers called my mom's cell phone. My mom told him what happened at the hospital. He told my mom that he would personally take care of these girls (don't forget that he was a witness to the accident). He said, and I quote, "THESE GIRLS ARE A THORN IN MY SIDE AND IN

In Jamie's Words

EVERYONE'S SIDE FOR THAT MATTER! HOPEFULLY THEY WILL MEET THEIR MATCH WHEN THEY HIT MIDDLE SCHOOL, BECAUSE WHAT GOES AROUND COMES AROUND!" He then gave my mom his home phone number and told her if we had any more problems to feel free to call him.

As soon as spring break was over I went back to school with a tube of A&D in my backpack and a broken heart! My mom went to the school at 10:30 am and spoke with Mr. Myers outside because there was a fire drill and most of the school had to stand out front. Well, if you're thinking that Mr. Myers took care of it, you're WRONG! I thought that I really could trust him. I was so let down and disappointed in him and so were my parents. We could not believe that he too let us down. He gave us his word that he would fix this.

A few days later I went to the bathroom in school and saw my name scrawled onto the wall in purple ink. I went back to the classroom and told Mr. Dickson. That afternoon a few girls from Mr. Myers' class came to me and told me that Betty had left the

In Jamie's Words

classroom with a purple marker in her pocket. I told the teachers what I had been told. They told me that they knew I didn't do it and they said that they were going to let the principal handle it. DID THEY SAY THE PRINCIPAL? YEAH, RIGHT! SHE'LL REALLY GET THE JOB DONE!

That night, my parents called Mr. Myers at home and discussed this with him in detail. He went on to say that he's sure that Betty will get what she deserves one day and that it'll be coming around soon for her. What kind of a joke was this? We were waiting for fate to kick in now! What kind of education was I really getting in this joke of a school? I'll tell you. I was learning how to have a broken heart most of the time. I was learning to never trust anyone, and I was learning that I had to fight for who I was!

The next day the principal called a 5th grade meeting in the gym. She told all the 5th graders that if she found out who wrote on the bathroom wall, they would lose their graduation privileges such as picture taking and yearbook signing. Didn't she already know who wrote on the bathroom wall? I mean I did tell the teacher and

In Jamie's Words

the assistant principal who did it, so what was she waiting for? Oh, I get it. She was trying to look like she was a principal in charge so she called a 5th grade meeting that really was to just blow smoke up our butts. On April 30th, my mom went back to school to speak to Mr. Myers regarding the bathroom wall incident only to be told again that there was nothing he could do!

May 12th was Philomena's birthday party. I really didn't want to go. It was at her house and all the bullies were going. So, I decided to tell her that I didn't want to go because I didn't want any more problems. As a result of me saying NO to the party, I had to endure more abusive behavior from the bullies. How dare I not want to go to the party? Did I think that I was better than those girls? Give me a break! Now I couldn't even make a decision about not wanting to be a part of the abuse-I was still going to be abused for it. Needless to say, Philomena's party was a total flop. Supposedly everyone was fighting and crying and there was no adult supervision. Sound like my kind of party? All I can say is thank God I said NO!

In Jamie's Words

On May 16th, Josephine, Philomena, and her friend Mora started to make fun of me. They would call me "B****" every chance they got! At the time, there were several witnesses to the name-calling including one mutual friend I had who went to Mr. Dickson as well as the principal with the girls' names.

That evening was a concert at the middle school so I was rushing to get ready. We stepped out to go to the mall to get a white shirt for the concert and when we got home there was a message on our answering machine from Philomena calling from Josephine's phone number. We identified the number from our caller I.D. I didn't return the call. I had just gone all day with these nasty girls and now they're calling my house to harass me? My dad brought me to the middle school with my brother. My mom and little sister stayed home because my sister felt sick. My dad brought me to the music room where everyone was waiting before they went on stage. The music teacher was in the room trying to get everyone organized for the show. My dad had walked away with my brother to find their seats when I was approached by Philomena, Josephine, Mora and

91

In Jamie's Words

another girl named Stella. Stella had been left back so she was one of the older ones in the school. She was also the one that the bullies went to for back up! The girls started to verbally abuse me. I told them to go away, that it didn't matter what they had to say. Then, the girls stood behind Stella while she threatened to beat me up after the show. She told me that I better shut up or she would shut me up! I told her to stop bothering me. Stella said, "You think you're so tough? We'll see just how tough you are!" With that, the music teacher overheard what was going on and she told me to come stand by her. I gladly walked away from these girls. I was hoping that maybe they would get in trouble for their behavior by the music teacher, but that didn't happen.

During the concert Stella and Josephine stood behind me as we were singing and they kept pulling my hair. They pulled the ponytail holder out while we were all singing. Then they would go back to pulling my hair. My dad could see that there was something wrong from the audience. He saw my face. After the show he quickly went backstage to get me. He tried talking with the music

In Jamie's Words

teacher, but she was too busy so we left. I was very upset all the way home. I couldn't believe what was going on. How could this just continuously happen every day without anyone getting in trouble? We had witnesses to most of the happenings but yet no one wanted to help us.

At 9:39 pm. that night right after the show, the phone rang at my house. I had just gotten out of the shower. My mom saw in the caller I.D. that it was Josephine again. My mom came into the bathroom and said "I'll pick up the phone and talk to Josephine while your father picks up a different phone to listen in." My mom answered the phone and it was Philomena asking to speak with me. My mom told her to hang on while she got me. As soon as I said hello, Philomena said "JAMIE, WHY ARE YOU RATTING US OUT?" Then she said "WE DON'T LIKE RATS AND WE'RE GONNA GET YOU TO STOP!" At that point all I had said was hello; my parents had heard the whole thing. My mom said to Philomena "THIS IS JAMIE'S MOM AND I HEARD THE THREAT YOU MADE!" My mom told them that they had to stop

In Jamie's Words

harassing me and that they were going to call the police and report the incident. Philomena said "OKAY, WE'LL STOP and WE'LL LEAVE JAMIE ALONE!" My mom hung up and immediately called the police. My mom spoke with someone in the Crimes Bureau who said that he would leave the information with a detective who would contact me within 24 hrs.

The next day I went to school and my mom parked on the side of the building and knocked on Mr. Dickson's outside door. When he answered he had a total attitude with my mother. He told her that he had already received a phone call from another parent and how dare my mom threaten another kid. Boy, was this getting ugly! First the threats, then all the lies!! My mom told Mr. Dickson that that wasn't the way it went at all. She went on to tell him what happened and his answer was "A PARENT'S GOTTA DO WHAT A PARENT'S GOTTA DO! I'LL TRY TO KEEP JAMIE SEPARATE FROM THE GIRLS BUT THAT'S IT!" My mom told him that she was going to hold him personally responsible for not protecting me and he said that he really didn't care! *My mom told him that one day he will eat those words because one day his daughter will be bullied and he'll be in the same position! Can you imagine being threatened by 11 year old brats? Having them try to destroy your life? Well, they tried but didn't succeed! The funny thing is that the police department told us that Philomena's house was a frequent stop for domestic violence and Josephine's house was a frequent stop for drug dealing!*

NOW WHO'S GOT THE LAST LAUGH?

On May 17th, at 10:30 am, my mom met another parent at the elementary school. Beatrice was a mutual friend of mine and Philomena's, so when her mom heard what happened she wanted to help out by going to the principal with my mom. When they met at the school office, the office manager was very rude. She told my mom and Beatrice's mom that the principal was too busy to talk to them and that they would have to come back later when it was more convenient for her. They had gone back to the school at approximately 1:00 pm. When they went into the principal's office my mom said that the principal made NO eye contact with my

In Jamie's Words

mother what so ever. The conversation was rather brief and absolutely nothing was accomplished. When the situation about the middle school concert was discussed, she said that it didn't matter to her! Oh, so now nothing that happens to me matters in that school? Pretty sad, don't you think?

On Friday, May 18, 2006, my mom dropped me off at school early for a bagel breakfast with the chorus group and the music teacher. As soon as I walked into the cafeteria Stella was standing on the risers and said "HEY B***H!" So, I walked over to the corner of the room to put my backpack down and then I turned to her and said "HEY STELLA, WHY DON'T YOU GO HOME AND STUDY INSTEAD OF CALLING ME NAMES AND CURSING AT ME, THIS WAY YOU WON"T GET LEFT BACK AGAIN!" Everyone laughed! They couldn't believe that I answered the biggest bully back with a great comment. Stella went running into the principal's office to tell her what I said. Soon, the principal came into the cafeteria and said, "JAMIE, I KNOW THAT YOU'VE BEEN THROUGH A LOT IN THIS SCHOOL, BUT IT'S NOT

In Jamie's Words

NICE TO SAY MEAN THINGS TO PEOPLE!" I was upset all day. How could I get accused of saying mean things to people, when it was actually the first time I had opened my mouth to defend myself in 3 years!

At the end of the day my dad came to pick me up at school. He was picking me and my brother up. When I came to him I had tears in my eyes. I told my dad what happened and he was absolutely FURIOUS! My dad went running across the walkway screaming at the principal in front of all the kids, teachers and parents. My dad said that it was about time that we got a new principal along with new rules to stop bullying. He told her that she runs the school like a CIRCUS! He also expressed how the school had become an UNSAFE ENVIRONMENT! The whole time that my dad was yelling at her she kept saying, "PLEASE, CAN'T WE GO INSIDE?" My father agreed to step inside the school where he continued to tell the principal *WE SEND OUR CHILDREN TO SCHOOL TO LEARN, NOT TO BE BULLIED AND HARASSED BY OTHER KIDS, MOST OF ALL, NOT TO HAVE THEIR*

SPIRITS CRUSHED BY A PRINCIPAL THAT WOULD RATHER PRAISE THE BULLY AND REPRIMAND THE GOOD CHILD THAN PUNISH THE BULLY AND HAVE PEACE AND HARMONY WITHIN THE SCHOOL!"

CAN YOU BELIEVE THE SCHOOL MOTTO IS "PEACE, PRIDE AND RESPECT?"

Once again my parents went to the district office to make another complaint about the principal. If you haven't already noticed, my parents' nerves were SHOT!

On May 31, 2007, my mom called the "Center for School Safety" in Albany New York. She told them in detail what was going on with the school district and principal. They put my mom in touch with a gentleman named Mr. Jones. When my mom finally got in touch with Mr. Jones, he was surprised and shocked to hear all the incidents that had been going on in the school. He made some notes and also made some phone calls to the principal. For the most part, the principal was ignoring his phone calls, but Mr. Jones was persistent. Finally, Mr. Jones got through to the principal who told him that I had some trouble keeping friends, but then again, so do all 5th graders. Okay, so what does that mean? He went on to discuss my safety and well being. In the end, the outcome was that the principal told him that if he called her again that she would consider it harassment and file a harassment lawsuit. Mr. Jones went on to tell her that it was his job to follow through and it wouldn't be considered harassment at all! Mr. Jones called my mom afterwards to tell her how irrational the principal was. He said that the best thing we could do is get out of that school, including moving my brother and sister too. He also told my mother that she needed to find other families with similar complaints about the principal so that maybe together we could have her removed as principal.

On Friday, June 1st, 2007, my mom went to the school office to request a *FOIL Form* so that she would be able to obtain my personal records from the school. The office manager and the secretary had no idea what a *FOIL Form* was. A *FOIL Form* stands for FREEDOM OF INFORMATION LAW. This document allows you to retrieve your child's personal information in their school file.

In Jamie's Words

My mom wanted to see my file to see if anything had been indicated in it regarding the bullying. The principal came out of her office and asked my mom what it was that she needed because there weren't any FOIL Forms. She allowed my mom to inspect my personal file which had very little in it and then asked "Do you need anything else?" My mom told the principal that she needed copies of all of my weekly progress reports. The principal called Mr. Dickson and asked him to get any progress reports that he had so that my mom could have them. He came back to the office with only one. It was from May 7th, 2007, which showed that I had to FOCUS MORE! When my mom asked where all of the other progress reports were, Mr. Dickson said that he threw them out. Now why would a teacher discard progress reports if they originally had to be signed by a parent and returned the next day? Did my progress reports show that I was struggling all along? Did they show that I had focusing issues since the beginning? OF COURSE THEY DID! That's why he refused to show them to my mom again and give her a copy. So

In Jamie's Words

basically, the school violated my rights again to have all copies of reports!

Then the principal said to my mother "JAMIE IS A REALLY GOOD KID AND I'M SORRY SHE HAD TO GO THROUGH ALL OF THIS! WE SHOULD TRY TO MAKE HER LAST FEW WEEKS LEFT HERE IN FIFTH GRADE ENJOYABLE!" My mom told her that it was a shame that I had to have so much turmoil all these years for no reason! All that had to be done was to punish the girls for doing all the harassing. The principal said that she never had enough proof. She told my mom that she would like to settle this amicably. My mom told her that I was damaged mentally and physically beyond AMICABLY! The principal then went on to say that IF WE WERE TO GO DOWN THE ROAD SHE THINKS THAT WE'RE GOING DOWN, THEN SHE FEELS CONFIDENT IN HERSELF! My mom told her - "GOOD, BECAUSE YOU'RE GOING TO NEED IT, I HAVE ALL MY DUCKS IN A ROW AND ALL THE PROOF I NEED AND I'M EXTREMELY CONFIDENT THAT WHAT YOU DID

In Jamie's Words

TO MY DAUGHTER AND WHAT THE SCHOOL ALLOWED TO HAPPEN WAS WRONG!"

NOT ONLY WERE MY MOM'S DUCKS IN A ROW, BUT THEY WERE ARMED AND READY FOR WAR!

My mom left pretty angry after that. She couldn't believe that in one breath the principal felt so bad about what happened that she felt confident in herself to go down an ugly road and defend what she did. What the HELL is that all about? You feel confident that you hurt a child? That makes you feel good inside? You think that my mom and dad should consider going down a different road and maybe thank her for all of the abuse? NEVER! We weren't going down without a fight! I didn't care if other families got involved with their stories or not. My parents didn't care either. All we cared about was getting our lives back.

On June 11th, 2007 my dad went to the school because I failed another math test. When he got there, they called me down to meet with them. My dad and I met with Mr. Dickson and the principal. My dad started to discuss the fact that I had been bullied

In Jamie's Words

for so long that I couldn't concentrate and that's why I failed. At that point the principal said that she didn't care what the reason was that I failed, even if it was because of all the bullying! She then got up and walked out of her office. How could she not care if I failed or passed? All I kept thinking was that I would never get these years back. How would I ever get another chance educationally? I'm only in 5th grade and the best school years I have had were kindergarten and first grade. How would I ever make friends? All the kids knew what was going on. There was no chance of me bonding with anyone.

Honestly, who could I trust? I had this one friend who I thought I was close with. My mom was really close with her mom. I had never seen my mom have a friendship with anyone like the one she had with Cindy. I would go to Cindy's house a lot and Barbie and I would work on designing a kid's magazine. It was so much fun. I really loved it. Then, Barbie started to hang out with Carol. That's when the friendship ended. Not only did the friendship end with us, but also with my mom and Cindy. My mom was sooooo

In Jamie's Words

hurt. She couldn't believe that Cindy would allow her daughter to hang out with Carol knowing the situation. Why would she risk such a close friendship with my mom just so her daughter could befriend a bully? Needless to say, whatever the reason, the friendship ended!

This just goes to show you how some parents will go to any extreme to make their child fit in no matter who they hurt! All I have to say is, I hope Barbie's happy with the friends that she has chosen and the choices that she has made!

On June 11th, 2007, my dad called Mr. Jones to see what happened and he said that he sent the principal an email but she didn't respond. He told my dad to give him another day or two to get in touch with her and then we would talk. The next day, I was so upset about the principal's behavior that I didn't want to go to school. My mom called the school and explained to the secretary that due to the principal's attitude and non-caring ways that I wouldn't be going to school that day. On June 13th, Mr. Jones called and said that he spoke with the principal and she said that I was a good kid. She said that I never caused any trouble, but had some problems keeping friends. She then corrected herself and said that most kids at this age go through friends quickly. Now didn't we hear something similar to this last time Mr. Jones spoke with the principal? I guess she's at a loss for words, so she needs to say the same thing repeatedly.

Father's Day was June 17th, and the police officer had finally returned our call from a little over a month ago regarding the threats over the phone and the internet. Don't you think that was ridiculous on the police department's part? I mean, I could have been DEAD! You waste all this time and there wasn't anyone else that could have called to take care of the complaint? Supposedly the officer was injured on the job, so she took time off. So, I guess that's my problem now! Don't you think that the precinct should have put another detective on the case? I guess my family and I are just supposed to go with the flow on this one too? Anyway, the officer listened to the story from my mother and then contacted the girls' parents. I believe the officer also spoke with the principal. After speaking with everyone the officer got a subpoena to try to retrieve the instant message off of AIM. In the end there was nothing that the officer could do. The subpoena didn't help because the document wasn't saved on my hard drive. The officer refused to drag these kids through Family Court and she refused to issue an Appearance Ticket that would have brought them through probation. So we were back at square one again.

The next day, all the parents who were called by the police officer were in the principal's office. Apparently they were discussing the phone call they received from the officer. I was also told that the principal had disclosed the fact that I was in counseling and that I was CRAZY! Who gave her the right to judge me after what she had put me through? How dare she violate my rights and tell people that I'm in therapy? I'm in therapy because of what she did to me and what she allowed! Needless to say, that day was horrible for me in school!

In Jamie's Words

CHAPTER SIX

6th GRADE "The Spotted Feather"

Over the summer my mom and dad spoke with the middle school guidance counselors and requested that I be put on a different team than the girls that were bothering me. She agreed to do her best to keep me away from them.

It was my first day of middle school. My mom was taking me to a different bus stop in the morning because I didn't want to take the bus from my corner since Amelia used it. I also wanted to

In Jamie's Words

use this other bus stop because my two best friends were there, Victoria and Katherine. I looked forward to seeing them every morning, along with one of my other friends Kristy who was on that bus too. It felt good knowing that I had some friends on the bus. It seemed okay, even though the new bus route was about a mile away and was a bit of an inconvenience. But, as you have already read, this whole school nightmare has been a total inconvenience, so what difference did another a mile make?

The first couple of weeks seemed to be calm. Some occasional stares and dirty looks, but for the most part no one really did anything too bad until September 27th. I was in one of my classes with Halley, one of the mutual friends of Amelia. Halley told me that she needed to talk to me about something very important. She told me that she was upset with Amelia because she started a "HATE CLUB" against me. She was angry that she was being forced to join this club against her will in order to hurt me!

I couldn't believe it! I asked Halley, "Are you sure that Amelia and Carol and some of the other girls were getting together

In Jamie's Words

to hurt me?" She said yes! I got very upset! I asked Halley to please come to the guidance counselor's office with me and tell her what was going on, and she said yes! I said "THANK GOD!" We both went down there together and spoke with Mrs. Thompson. She seemed to be happy that I had a witness that came forward, and she thanked her for that. GOD FORBID SHE WOULD HAVE TAKEN MY WORD FOR IT! She told Halley that she did the right thing. I knew Halley did the right thing. Anything could've happened to me if that hate club would have got enough kids in it to hurt me!

Amelia got In School Suspension. I was very happy that she finally got some sort of punishment. It was long overdue, don't you think? But what about the other girls involved? How come they didn't get punished? Amelia may have thought up this HATE CLUB idea, but she's definitely not smart enough to carry it out alone! To the best of my knowledge, no one else was punished because of the HATE CLUB!

The next day, I really didn't want to go to school. I was nervous about this whole Hate Club thing. All I kept thinking was –

In Jamie's Words

what if all the other kids involved still tried to hurt me? What if they had a weapon on them? I was making myself so sick to my stomach. My mom kept trying to get me ready for school, but I was just moving really slow because I was overcome with *FEAR AND ANXIETY!* I finally agreed to go to school, but I wasn't happy! My mom put my brother and little sister in her truck along with me, and went to the bus stop - only to see that I had missed the bus. My mom turned the corner and headed for the school. As soon as she pulled out on the main road she wound up behind Amelia's bus. Would you believe that Amelia got the whole back of the bus to turn around and look at me and my mom and give us the finger? **Once again, here is another example of the disrespect of an ignorant child!** I guess that Amelia has a lot of pull with the other LOSERS on the bus! Honestly, if I saw someone giving another person the finger, I wouldn't chime in especially if it were a parent. I guess it all has to do with the way you were raised! I wasn't raised to be disrespectful. On the contrary, I was raised to respect my elders and my peers!

In Jamie's Words

Nevertheless, my mom dropped me off at school and went back home. After that, she went back up to the middle school and spoke with Mr. Morani about what took place on the bus and who the kids were that were involved. Then my mom told Mr. Morani about the whole HATE CLUB incident from the prior day because she wasn't sure if he knew. Mr. Morani wasn't sure of the HATE CLUB incident. He told my mom that he wasn't in that day! Of course he wasn't! That's why my mom took the time to explain it to him. You see, if you haven't guessed it by now- the right hand doesn't know what the left hand is doing in this school!

Later that afternoon, my mom touched base with Mrs. Thompson, the sixth grade guidance counselor, to see what had transpired with the bus incident. She said that most of the kids who were involved were called down to the office and she thought a phone call went home.

What do you mean YOU THINK THAT A PHONE CALL WENT HOME? You mean you don't know? If a phone call did go home, what else happened? Did they get punished or were they just

In Jamie's Words

warned? I guess we'll never know. Idiots with Cracker Jack diplomas run this school! The only thing we did find out was that Amelia could pretty much give anyone the finger and get other kids to chime in with her without getting punished! I love it, don't you? This school isn't teaching anyone anything except how to bully and be disrespectful! Is this what every school district is made of? Or do some school districts care about the quality of a child's education? *I think that this school should hand out clown shoes and red rubber noses, because that's all that's going to come out of this school unless they do something to fix their methods of teaching and disciplining!* It's very sad to think that school district and the superintendent would stand behind the principal and assistant principal and **WATCH A CHILD CRUMBLE RIGHT IN FRONT OF THEM!** *SHAME ON YOU!*

For the next few weeks Amelia would repeatedly stand near my locker with her *"POSSE"* as she put it. Her so-called *"POSSE"* included Carol, Betty and a few other girls. These girls were totally getting off on the fact that they were intimidating me or at least

In Jamie's Words

trying to! It was amazing, like clockwork, every morning they would talk to kids near my locker just so they could stare at me or say things to me as I walked by.

Finally, I went back to Mrs. Thompson and told her what they were doing. The next day Mrs. Thompson stood in the hallway near my locker and observed it for herself. She went over to them and told them to break it up and go to class and not to stand anywhere near my locker again. Well, I guess I should have been happy with that outcome? How come a phone call still didn't go home? ***WASN'T IT PHONE CALL WORTHY?*** I guess not! I guess that giving them a verbal warning was enough for her! It's so sad, don't you think? I mean by now everyone knew what was going on. I was becoming a laughing stock of the school because these bullies could do whatever they wanted and pretty much get away with it. Over the next few months, every time Amelia and her ***"POSSE"*** would pass me in the hall they had some kind of comment. I tried not to pay attention to them. I just kept telling myself that they were just a waste of time and they weren't worth my energy to even

In Jamie's Words

answer them back. ***Wasn't I worth anything? Didn't they care that I couldn't focus? Why couldn't someone punish all of these girls so that they would leave me alone for good? They didn't care about me or my feelings, or my education, or my parents' wasted tax dollars, or the effect that all of this bullying would have on me and my family! All they cared about were themselves! They couldn't see that I was slipping through the cracks!***

If this wasn't bad enough, my mom spoke with Mrs. Hemmingway, who was tutoring me, who told my mom that she felt really sorry for me and the situation, but she wasn't going to participate in the tattling on the school conduct of the principal and the teachers involved. So, what does that mean exactly? Even though she had already voiced her opinion of the principal to my mom, and told my mom in detail about how the principal does a lot of underhanded things, she wasn't willing to step up to the plate to do the right thing? See, that's what wrong with society! People see with their own eyes, but speak only what they want, not what is right. If it were their child, things would probably be different. Mrs.

In Jamie's Words

Hemmingway never had children, so she only knows what goes on in a classroom with kids not at home. My parents had paid her $50 a week to tutor me over the course of 2 years. If you think about it, that adds up to a lot of money and a lot of time spent in order to have me stay focused and pass my tests! It's too bad because we had a lot of respect for her. The way my parents looked at this was that if she wasn't willing to speak, then we'd just have to subpoena her! Too bad we never taped all of her conversations, but in the end, we believed the truth would come out!

In Jamie's Words

CHAPTER SEVEN

THE DOMINO EFFECT

While I was fighting my own battles in the middle school, all hell was breaking loose for my dad, brother and little sister in the elementary school! You see, we waited until I graduated 5th grade to serve the Notice of Claim (lawsuit) on the school district regarding the elementary school, the principal and all teachers involved in my bullying and defamation. We figured that this was the safest route for us to take to ensure my graduation process of 5th grade. The other reason was because my grandfather was very sick with Multiple Myeloma, which is cancer of the bone marrow. We watched him fade quickly since this was a battle that he had been fighting for the past 7 years. I tried not to discuss my problems with him because he had enough to worry about and I didn't want him to worry about me.

On November 12th, 2007, my grandfather died. The pain of losing him was almost too much to bear. With everything that had been going on, my family and I were really distraught. He was such a good man who treated everyone with the highest respect. He had so much dignity even when he was fading away. I think this is why my mom and dad chose to follow through with the lawsuits and the character complaints because of how strong and focused my Poppy was and how dedicated he was to our family. All I could hope for is that my Poppy was watching over me and my family and that I was making him proud! We missed and loved him and no matter what the school district and principal put us through, we would rise above it!

119

In Jamie's Words

The amazing thing was what the SICK principal decided to put our family through as a result of us filing the lawsuit and naming her in it! Maybe she thought that we were more vulnerable since the death of my grandfather? Maybe she thought that we were ready to crack. *Here's a word of advice to you, Ms. Van Dyke: we weren't ready to give up just yet, we were ready to fight you with whatever strength we had left, even if it killed us! You know the saying "What doesn't kill you makes you stronger." Well that's us!*

It was December 6th and my dad went to the elementary school to pick up my brother from 4th grade and my sister from kindergarten. He parked in the handicapped spot on the side of the school where he had always parked, displaying his handicap permit on his rear view mirror. He proceeded to get out of his car and walk down the sidewalk toward the school when the principal, Ms. Van Dyke, approached him and told him that he had to get off the sidewalk and walk a different route to get Danny and Lindsey. My dad told Ms. Van Dyke that his back was hurting him and that he really needed to sit on the bench and wait for his kids to exit the

In Jamie's Words

school. Ms. Van Dyke refused to allow him to walk on the sidewalk and demanded that he take the longest route to get to the front of the school to get the kids. My dad obeyed and walked the other way, which was the longest route around the buses and the driveway in order to get my brother and sister, while other parents who weren't handicapped were allowed to walk on the sidewalk. When he returned to his vehicle, Ms. Van Dyke was waiting for him at his car. She proceeded to tell my dad that he was *A SECURITY RISK!*

My dad was really angry! He wanted to know what kind of a security risk he was. She wouldn't answer him. My brother and sister were watching this whole thing and getting very upset. They couldn't understand why the principal was behaving this way. My sister started to cry because she was getting very upset with the way Ms. Van Dyke was speaking to my dad. My dad chose to walk away and get everyone in the car and go home. He didn't want Lindsey to get more upset so he decided to leave before it got worse. When he got home he went on the computer and looked up THE AMERICANS WITH DISABILITIES ACT and THE US

In Jamie's Words

DEPARTMENT OF EDUCATION, OFFICE FOR CIVIL RIGHTS. My dad got all of the information pertaining to our situation and started to draft a letter to them.

FROM THIS MOMENT ON WE KNEW THAT IT WAS GOING TO BE WAR!

The next day, my mom, dad and I went to the elementary school to pick up my brother and sister. My mom was driving her truck while my dad lay down in the back seat so that he wouldn't be noticed. As we approached the school we noticed that there was a security vehicle parked illegally in the handicapped spot that my dad usually parked in. Standing next to the spot was a security guard as well as Ms. Van Dyke. It was like they were waiting to have an argument with my dad. My mom pulled up behind the illegally parked car and I got out and walked right down the sidewalk to pick up my brother and sister and no one stopped me! As I returned with my siblings they were still standing there staring at my mom in her truck. My mom came prepared with a camera and took a picture of

In Jamie's Words

Ms. Van Dyke standing right near our vehicle while my dad watched the whole thing through the back tinted windows.

Amazing isn't it? She got security to stand with her so that she could try to harass and intimidate my dad. How come the guard was allowed to park in the handicapped spot? He's not handicapped. Why didn't he just pull up and double park? My dad is legitimately handicapped and he was prevented from parking in this spot because the principal wanted to harass him! The best part was that I walked down the sidewalk right in front of them and no one said anything or stopped me! There were even teachers outside on the sidewalk, but no one seemed to mind that I was walking on it. How come? *WAS IT DISCRIMINATION AGAINST MY DAD?* **YOU DECIDE!**

For the next few weeks my mom was picking up my brother and sister at school. Everything seemed to be pretty calm. No one bothered her or tried to stop her from walking down the sidewalk. How come they didn't bother her? At one point, my mom had walked around the buses and was waiting near the flagpole with

In Jamie's Words

some of the other mothers when Ms. Van Dyke came out and stood in the middle of the crosswalk and stared at my mother and laughed. My mom laughed right back at her and stared her down as well. The whole time, all my mom kept thinking was what a shallow and self absorbed person she was. How could the principal be pleased with her disgraceful behavior? Did she go to work every morning with a smile on her face because she thought that she was going to harass my family today?

A few days later, my dad drove to the school to pick up Danny and Lindsey. As he approached the side of the school to park in his usual handicapped spot he saw that there were 3 security guards as well as the principal. When they saw my dad pulling up to the spot, they all went into attack mode. He hadn't even turned the car off when they *surrounded his vehicle! The principal, along with one of the security guards, placed their hands on my dad's driver side door and refused to let him out of his vehicle!* My dad forced his way out and got my brother and sister.

In Jamie's Words

On December 21st, my dad and I drove to the elementary school to pick up my brother and sister. My dad parked in a handicapped spot on the side of the school. We both got out of the car and walked down the sidewalk and stayed near the entrance of the school due to snowy conditions outside. We waited there until my brother and sister came out of school. After they came out, we walked down the side walk and headed back to our car when we were approached by the principal. *YOU HAD TO SEE HER WALKING TOWARDS US WITH HER BOWED LEGS, FRUMPY DRESS AND HER MANLY STATURE! WOW, WHAT A SHOW STOPPER!* She insisted that we turn around and walk all the way back around the buses in the ice and snow in order to get back to our car. My dad told her that the path she suggested was too icy and he would be at risk of falling. I also told her that there were plenty of other parents walking the same route that I had chosen and she was allowing them to continue on. As I proceeded to walk away from her, she began to yell at me and my family. She said that we

In Jamie's Words

were all a security risk and that if we didn't obey her, she would call security! We just kept walking and ignoring her threats.

All I have to say is thank God it was Christmas break, because we all needed it!

My brother and sister returned to school after New Years. My mom had decided to pick them up for the next few weeks to see if it was going to make a difference again. Once again, everything seemed a little better until January 14, 2008. My dad went to the school to pick up Danny and Lindsey. He got out of his car and walked around the long way to get them so that there wouldn't be any problems with the principal. I guess that it really didn't matter which way he walked, because Ms. Van Dyke was still looking for an argument!

As my dad approached the vehicle with my brother and sister, he noticed that the principal was following close behind him. As Danny and Lindsey were getting into the car, Ms. Van Dyke demanded to see my father's handicapped permit. My dad tried to ignore her, but she was very persistent and demanded it! As my dad

In Jamie's Words

proceeded to get into the car to unhook it off of the rear view mirror Ms. Van Dyke went so far as to ***GRAB IT OUT OF HIS HANDS!*** My dad looked at her and said "Hey, what was that for?" ***SHE TURNED AROUND AND MUMBLED UNDER HER BREATH "STUPID JEW!"*** He stood there in disbelief, with my brother and sister listening to her defame and demean him! He couldn't believe his ears! ***How could this STUPID, IGNORANT, SHALLOW, PREJUDICED person be running an elementary school, teaching children right from wrong?*** At that point, my dad called my mom at work and told her what just happened. She put her coat on and closed up the deli early and sped to the school, while my dad called 911.

Once again this whole situation has cut into our lives so severely. ***It had hurt us MENTALLY, MORALLY, PHYSICALLY and FINANCIALLY!*** Can you imagine having to keep going up to a school for repeated problems like this and getting absolutely nowhere? Or, having the principal target you and your family the way Ms. Van Dyke did, as well as the district? The police came and

In Jamie's Words

started to take the police report from my dad. My mom pulled up just minutes later and when she did, Ms. Van Dyke was blocking the exit of the parking lot along with one of the security guards. She was standing there all annoyed with her arms crossed with this nasty look on her face. With that, my mom's cell phone rang. It was the elementary school superintendent Casey Kahn. She asked my mom to please not press charges against the principal. She said that it wasn't right for her to rip the handicapped permit out of my dad's hands and that whatever she mumbled under her breath wasn't professional. My mom told her that she was going to let the police write the report. My mom told Ms. Kahn that she was extremely disappointed in the school system and that the harassment had to stop! Ms. Kahn told my mom that she would like to quickly switch my brother and sister to one of the other elementary schools. She also wanted to have a meeting the following day. *WE WERE ALL EXTREMELY UPSET AND DISTRAUGHT ABOUT WHAT HAD JUST HAPPENED!*

In Jamie's Words

My mom and dad were absolutely furious. We realized at this point that it had become personal. The principal actually had the district send security guards to prevent my dad from parking in the handicapped spot, walking on the sidewalk, and having all of the same rights that the other parents had. We actually took photos of cars parked illegally in the handicapped parking spots and photos of other parents walking freely on the sidewalk in front of the school. It was at this time that we realized that we needed to hire a private investigator to document everything that we were experiencing, and photograph and videotape everything that was happening. We felt so betrayed! When I think about it now, I don't even know how we existed! What I mean is, I don't know how we even got up in the morning. How did my parents even get through the day?

On January 18th, my brother Danny was having lunch in the cafeteria of his elementary school. On a daily basis, he assisted a Special Ed girl named Heidi during lunch. My brother would help Heidi buy her lunch and help her cut up her food. Then, he would throw her garbage away. When lunch was over, he would sometimes

In Jamie's Words

take Heidi outside for recess or bring her back to her class. The whole time my brother was helping Heidi, he was with all the other kids from his class who had a Special Ed child to care for. My brother was really great with Heidi. He was extremely patient with her. This is why what I'm about to tell you is so disturbing!

My brother started to have some problems with some of the girls in his class. They would be really spiteful to him. Occasionally, some of his things would disappear from inside his desk or he would find some of his things broken. Anyway, they became very jealous of him and decided to make up a story about him hurting Heidi and spread it around the school! The main culprit was Wanda. Wanda decided to go over to one of the lunch teachers on duty and tell them *that **my brother Danny took Heidi into the girl's bathroom to look at her privates!*** The lunch teacher immediately questioned Danny about this issue. My brother didn't even know what he was talking about. He told the lunch teacher that he hadn't left the cafeteria at all and that he had several witnesses at the lunch table. My brother got very upset and couldn't believe that someone would be that vicious

In Jamie's Words

and cruel! The principal called him into the office and questioned him as well. He told her the same thing that he didn't leave the cafeteria at all. He said that he came in, sat Heidi down, went to buy her lunch and sat back down with her along with all of the other kids at the lunch table. He told the principal that it was all a lie and that someone was making it up to hurt him!

My brother went back to class and looked around to see who would do something like that. He saw Wanda and Kendra turning around and laughing at him. He asked the teacher if he could please go back down to the principal's office. When he got down there he asked Ms. Van Dyke if it was Wanda and Kendra who told her that story. The principal said that it was Wanda and that she did what she did because she was concerned for Heidi. My brother told Ms. Van Dyke that he is very kind to Heidi and that maybe she should question Heidi to see if anything like that was ever done to her by him. Ms. Van Dyke said that she didn't want to question Heidi because she didn't think that she was capable of answering her. Personally, I think that the real reason that she never questioned her

In Jamie's Words

was because she knew that the story wasn't real and she didn't want to frighten a Special Ed child! Later that day, my dad went to the school to pick up my brother and sister. When Danny came, out he immediately told my dad what happened. My dad was FUMING! My brother told me that he had never seen my dad that angry. He said it looked as if he were going to **EXPLODE!**

My dad went to Wanda's house and spoke to her mother. My dad was pretty direct and stated that her daughter insinuated that his son sexually harassed a Special Ed child. *He wanted to make sure that she understood the web of lies that her daughter created.* The mother stood at the door with her eyes popping out of her head in silence! My dad told her that if her daughter didn't go back into school the next day and tell the truth to the principal, he was going to the police to press charges!

The next day my mom went to the district office and filled out a Harassment Complaint Form against Wanda for starting a rumor like that. My dad called Ms. Kahn to make an appointment to discuss this problem with her and the next day, my mom and dad

In Jamie's Words

went to see her. She told them she knew that my brother didn't do that to Heidi. She said that for whatever reason this rumor was started it had no merit. Ms. Kahn said that Danny wasn't going to be punished because the story was false. My mom and dad asked if Wanda was going to get punished for what she did and Ms. Kahn said NO! Of course it was no, did we expect it to be yes? Did we expect the school to actually punish someone for defaming my family? The whole thing was such a joke! The whole school is a joke!

Maybe the school district should take a good look at this whole situation and decide to turn the elementary school into a school for comedians! Just think about how gratifying it would be to see all of Ms. Van Dyke's students following in her footsteps! Maybe one day they will all be on stage doing a stand up show!

My mom and dad decided at this time that they needed to hire a private investigator to assist them. My mom had a customer at the deli who was a retired police officer who did investigation work on the side. She discussed the school situation with him and he was eager to help. So, my mom and dad got started right away with this investigator, Philip. Philip would go to the elementary school and set up surveillance cameras in his car so that he could video tape people walking down to sidewalk freely without security or the principal bothering them. He also observed teachers walking past my father's car and pointing at it and making a joke. Once, Philip observed a teacher come up behind my dad and make funny gyrations behind his back! Philip knew that this was a situation that was definitely discussed between the principal and all of the teachers. It had looked as if all of the teachers were instructed to DEFAME MY DAD IN PUBLIC! Philip also saw that cars without valid handicapped permits were allowed to park in the handicapped spots.

After gathering enough evidence against the school and the principal, my dad decided to write a letter to THE UNITED STATES DEPARTMENT OF EDUCATION, OFFICE OF CIVIL RIGHTS! He had already started to draft a letter a few weeks back, but now it was time to really get focused and send this letter out. In the mean time, my brother was trying to get through each day without drama. It was difficult because Wanda and Kendra were very mean to Danny. If my brother would leave to go to the bathroom, these girls would go through his desk and steal his pencils and pencil sharpener. One day, my brother saw Wanda using a pencil sharpener that looked just like his. Danny then went to take his sharpener out of his desk and that's when he realized that Wanda had stolen his. He was so upset because my grandparents had bought him a whole set of matching school supplies that were really nice and my brother cherished them because my grandfather had just died! My brother went over to Wanda and asked her where she got the sharpener and she didn't answer. Danny went over to the teacher and told her what Wanda did. The teacher asked Wanda if she took my brother's school stuff and she said no! The teacher then told my brother that maybe Wanda had the same pencils and sharpener that he did. My brother started to get really uptight. He told the teacher that he wanted his things back right now! She told him that she really didn't know what to do about it since Wanda said that the stuff was hers. My mom picked up my brother and sister that day from school. When Danny came outside he looked visibly upset! My mom asked him what happened and he told her. When they got home, my mom looked at all my brother's things to see exactly what was stolen. After taking a good look at everything they saw that it was 2 pencils and the matching sharpener. The next morning my mom and my brother went to the district office to see the superintendent.

The secretary brought my mom right down to his office, while my brother sat in the waiting room. Mr. Butterman greeted my mom at his door and said ***"WOW, DID WE EVER MEET BEFORE, BECAUSE I WOULD'VE REMEMBERED YOU."*** My mom shook his hand and told him that she was there to discuss my brother's situation, not his sex drive! My mom was real direct with Mr. Butterman. She told him that it didn't matter how many items were stolen out of Danny's desk, she wanted them back! She asked him to get on the phone and call over to Ms. Van Dyke and fix this problem. My mom demanded that he make the call right in front of her and Mr. Butterman did. After that my mom told him what a disgrace the elementary school was and how it was a FREE FOR ALL!

When my mom was finished with Mr. Butterman, he looked as if he was ready for a rubber room! Afterwards, she took my brother back to school. As soon as he got into class he put his backpack down in the back of the room and went to the bathroom. When he got back, he went about his school work until it was recess. Danny went to his backpack with his friend to take out his football only to find that it was gone! My brother went to the teacher and told her that his football was gone. Her response was "Maybe you left it at home and thought that you put it in your backpack?" So, with that my brother and his friend walked away and went back into the classroom and decided to take matters into their own hands. They each started at a different end and one by one unzipped each kids backpack until they found the football! The football was in Kendra's backpack. At that point the boys went over to the teacher and told her that Kendra had stolen the football because they found it in her backpack. The teacher got angry at my brother for going into someone else's backpack, so my brother told her that he had to take matters into his own hands because she wasn't willing to do her job!

The next day my mom went back up to the district office and spoke with the middle school superintendent, Mr. Babble. She told him that she had been there the day before when she spoke with Mr. Butterman regarding kids being allowed to steal from her son and now these same kids stole his football out of his backpack when he went to the bathroom! Of course nothing was ever done about this situation. Not even a return phone call or a punishment for these girls!

When my mom got home she made some phone calls to other parents whose children were in that classroom to see if they had any items stolen. As it turns out, several children had their belongings stolen and there was never a consequence for the two girls! As a matter of fact, the school actually gave Wanda the privilege of taking care of Heidi, the Special Ed girl who she tried to ruin when she attempted to make up that rumor about my brother.

Now, on a daily basis Wanda would take Heidi to the lunch table and sit her down and get her lunch. The only thing was that Wanda was **ABUSIVE** to Heidi. She would twist her arm if she didn't listen. She would grab her by the wrist and squeeze it if she got up to talk to my brother. There were several witnesses who observed Wanda behaving like this, including Heidi who would run to my brother for help! My brother along with a few other boys went to the principal's office to tell her what Wanda was doing to Heidi. **UNFORTUNATELY FOR HEIDI, NOTHING WAS DONE TO CORRECT THIS SITUATION, SO THE ABUSE CONTINUED! The amazing thing was that Wanda was chosen to make Renaissance. Teachers would nominate kids that showed good character as well as having good grades which would make them eligible to receive a certificate for their acts of kindness and for showing PEACE, PRIDE and RESPECT!** *It's*

In Jamie's Words

almost hard to believe isn't it? Believe me I couldn't make this stuff up if I tried!

The stress was mounting and the tension was so thick for my brother in school and for my family at home! My mom and dad agreed to move my brother and sister to a new school within the district, but they were waiting for winter recess. They figured that this would be a good time to end one school and begin another after a long break! The only problem was that with all the stress and tension, could we all last until the break?

We had about a week left before winter recess when my dad started to feel really sick. *He felt like he was having a stroke!* My mom rushed home from work and took my dad, along with me, my brother and sister, to the hospital to see what was happening. When we arrived at the hospital, they immediately took my dad right in. They saw that his face was starting to become paralyzed and the lines on his forehead were starting to disappear. *They did some tests and saw that it wasn't a stroke, it was BELL'S PALSY! The whole left side of my father's face started to droop. His eye wouldn't*

In Jamie's Words

close and therefore it teared all day because it was getting dry. He couldn't drink from a glass because the water would pour out, so he had to drink from a straw. Even drinking from a straw was difficult because he lost the feeling on the left side of his tongue. He also couldn't hear out of his left ear. All he heard was crackling and a loud clicking in his ear. This whole ordeal had taken its toll on my mom, my dad and my family, but we weren't giving up!

My mom went to the school and spoke with the nurse, Mrs. Foster, and told her what happened to my dad. She was very upset for us. She had basically tried to convey several times to us that the situation at that elementary school was never going to change. The only way it would change was if we left the school. HOW SAD, DON'T YOU THINK, THAT IT HAD TO COME TO THIS - THAT NO ONE COULD MAKE IT RIGHT? THAT NO ONE COULD REACH OUT TO US AND HELP US IN OUR TIME OF NEED?

In Jamie's Words

It was such a mess, you have no idea! My dad was soooo sick. He developed a rash all over his body because of the high dose of Prednisone that the hospital had put him on. He would also break out in cold sweats due to the medication. This ultimately led to him developing Chronic Urticaria, which is when your immune system is compromised and you become allergic to yourself! He needed care all day and my mom had to work because we owned a deli. Our whole lives were turned upside down, all because of the principal and the school district. You see, this isn't just a story about bullying.

My mom would get us off to school and set my dad up for the rest of the day with medication, heating pads, lunch, drinks, etc. She hired someone to open up the deli at 5:00 am so that she could take care of us and my dad in the morning. Then she would leave the deli to come home at around 2:30pm to pick us up from school and drop us off at home, only to drive back to Oyster Bay, where our deli was located, to clean and lock up. By the time she came home, she was exhausted! Her life was chaos! She would cook dinner, get us in the shower, get us into bed and then try to take care of my

In Jamie's Words

father. The way we looked at this was that if it didn't kill us, it would make us stronger and honestly we weren't so sure that this wasn't going to kill us!

It had seemed as if the whole world had turned its back on us! We felt very helpless and alone. There were times I would hear my mom crying in her bathroom, asking God "Why?" How could the school allow these little kids to hurt a family like this? It was totally out of control! It was like a ride at the amusement park that wouldn't stop and kept spinning faster!

My brother and sister still had one week left before they changed schools. My mom had to continue to look at Ms. Van Dyke every day that week when she went to pick up my brother and sister. The crazy thing was that the janitor that my mom was feeding occasionally was told by Ms. Van Dyke to stay away from my brother and have no conversation with him. You see, the janitor was looking out for us while we were at lunch. He would make sure that no one bothered us. The sad part was that he listened to Ms. Van Dyke and turned his back on not only my brother but my mom too!

In Jamie's Words

At one point, my brother went up to him at lunch and asked him what was wrong. He replied by saying "Danny, go sit down before the principal sees me talking to you!" My brother was very hurt and confused. He couldn't understand why someone that was once protecting him was now turning his back on him. I remember feeling so hurt for my brother when that happened. I didn't know what to do or what to say to him to make it better. As for my mom, she would drop my brother and sister off at school at the side entrance of the school. When she was driving by, she would see the janitor on bus duty at the end of the school driveway and he would go out of his way to turn his back on her! She couldn't believe it! How could a man behave in that fashion to someone that had been so kind and generous to him? He's not a child that was about to get scolded for not obeying; he was a grown man that chose to turn his back on a family that had done nothing wrong!

It was February 12, 2008 and my brother and sister only had a few days left to go to that school. My mom took a half day off from the deli to go to my sister's class for 100th Day. The

In Jamie's Words

kindergarten class was having a party and my mom wanted to be there. She figured that she would say goodbye to the teacher and collect all of my sister's things. My mom signed in at the front desk at approximately 1:00pm. She went down to my sister's classroom for the party. The teacher was really happy to see my mom, but sad to know that she wasn't going to have Lindsey in her class much longer! It was about 3pm in the afternoon when my mom left the classroom with Lindsey. She walked back to the front desk and asked if they could call my brother down for early dismissal. My brother came down 5 minutes later and my mom signed them both out at 3:00pm, a bit earlier than regular dismissal time. She walked out the front door and turned down the sidewalk and headed toward her car. It was very cold out that day and there was a lot of snow coming down. She walked carefully down the sidewalk holding my sister's hand when she stopped briefly to say goodbye to a bus driver that she knew very well. Suddenly, she was approached from behind by the principal. Ms. Van Dyke put her arms apart really wide behind my brother and sister. She told my mom that she had to

In Jamie's Words

get off the sidewalk immediately! My mom told her NO! She started telling my mom that she was a "SECURITY RISK" and that she needed to get off of the sidewalk now! My mom told her that it was 15 minutes before school was ending and there was no reason to get off of the sidewalk. Well, Ms. Van Dyke didn't like that answer. *She decided to grab my brother's left arm and attempt to pull him off of the sidewalk. Fortunately, my brother is a really big kid and he really didn't budge. The bad news was that she was squeezing his arm so tight that she left black & blue fingerprints on his arm. The whole time this was going on, my mother was yelling at the principal to get her hands off of her son! When Ms. Van Dyke found she couldn't budge my brother she immediately grabbed my sister by the shoulders and squeezed them and lifted her up and forcefully moved her to another part of the sidewalk! My mom was absolutely FREAKING OUT!*

My mom told the principal that she was going to make sure that she didn't get away with what she had done! AT THAT VERY MOMENT MY MOTHER REALIZED THAT THE PRINCIPAL

146

In Jamie's Words

WAS TRYING TO PROVOKE HER INTO HITTING HER! My mom knew better than that! Honestly, I don't know how my mother didn't beat her to death! My mom's disposition is very kind and happy until someone does something to hurt one of us! That's why I am shocked that she didn't go crazy on her! I guess it showed how focused my mom really is on getting the JUSTICE that we all deserve for what was done! I also know that she was asking for God to give her the strength not to hit Ms. Van Dyke! My mom felt as though she had kept her hands clean for all this time and she wasn't about to dirty them now!

It's really amazing how Ms. Van Dyke could go out of her way to hurt a family like this. Personally, I think that it takes a lot more energy to be mean to someone than it does just to be kind. My mom always tells us that life is so short, so try to enjoy it to the fullest and be the best person that you can be! **I wonder what Ms. Van Dyke's mother told her when she was growing up? And who cares, right?** *FOR ALL WE KNOW, MS. VAN DYKE WAS RAISED BY A PACK OF WOLVES!*

In Jamie's Words

My mom agreed to turn around and head the other way off the sidewalk, but before she headed in the other direction the bus driver said "Anne, what the hell just happened?" My mom just looked at her with a very disgusted look on her face and said "Didn't you just see what happened?" After that she turned and took my sisters hand as my brother followed and headed the other way.

When my mom got to the car, she called my dad and told him what happened. She was so upset and distraught! When they got home, my mom called 911. She explained to the dispatcher what happened and they said that a police officer would be right over. The reason my mother didn't call the police from the school was because she felt like Ms. Van Dyke would turn the tables on her and she wanted to get my brother and sister back home where it was safe.

The police came quickly! When the officer got to the house he took a statement from my brother, my sister and then my mother. My brother rolled up his sleeve to show the officer where Ms. Van Dyke grabbed him. That's when we saw the black and blue finger prints on his arm! At the same time, my sister told the officer that Ms. Van Dyke hurt her shoulders and they felt really sore. My mom gave the officer the name and cell phone number of the bus driver so that he could contact her since she witnessed the whole thing.

The police officer left the house and went to the school to question the principal. After he left, my mother's next phone call was to CPS (Child Protective Services). My mom reported the assault on my brother and sister. Would you believe that even though they took the report, they weren't willing to follow up on it because they said that the school district had to reprimand the principal? **YEAH, RIGHT! Honestly, where's the justice?** If a parent did this to her own child and someone called CPS there would be a full investigation into it. How come when it's the school that's at fault, they want the school district to resolve it? The next day my mom called the pediatrician's office. She wanted to see if she could bring my brother and sister in to get their arms and shoulders looked at, due to the assault. The doctor's office made the appointment for the 2 days later.

In Jamie's Words

My mom also spoke with the detective regarding the bus driver who witnessed the whole incident. She said that she was looking into it and she would get back to my mom as soon as she spoke with her. My mom called the district office and left a message for Ms. Kahn. My mom wanted her to know what took place. She left her a message to please call her back ASAP! Later that day she called back and told my mom that tomorrow would be Danny and Lindsey's last day of school. My mom had no problem with moving my brother and sister a day early, but she wanted to discuss the circumstances revolving around the assault on my siblings. Ms. Kahn made it clear to my mom that she wasn't concerned about what happened; she just wanted to move Danny and Lindsey right away! Were they admitting that the principal was the reason it wasn't safe? If so, why is Ms. Van Dyke still the principal? How come no one listened to my cries for help? How come no one heard my voice? How come no one listened to my brother's cries? Were they falling upon deaf ears? Personally this whole ordeal really took a toll on my brother. My little sister was able to manage it a little better, I think because she was so confused about what was going

on.

In the mean time, my dad started his acupuncture treatment

for his Bell's palsy. So on top of everything else, we still had to

keep the focus on helping my dad get better. There was so much

turmoil going on in our home as well as in school. We honestly

didn't know how to manage all of it!

The next day was my brother and sister's first day of school.

The ridiculous part was that they were going to go to school for one

day and then have a break all week for winter recess. The whole

thing was terrible! My mom spoke with Ms. Kahn that morning and

she said to meet in the office at 9:30am. She figured that it would be

easier to walk to the classrooms if there weren't a herd of kids in the

hallways.

So, my mom, dad, grandmother, sister and brother arrived at

the new school at 9:30 and met the new principal along with Ms.

Kahn. My brother was happy to be in a safer environment, but my

sister was devastated! They brought Lindsey to her classroom first.

In Jamie's Words

She was crying and didn't want to go in. My mom took her hand and walked with her into the class and sat with her. She was so upset. She didn't want to let go of my mother. The teacher came over and spoke with her and introduced her to all the kids. My mom stayed with her for a while until she calmed down. The teacher sat her next to a girl who was going to be on the same bus as her. They started talking a little and Lindsey stopped crying.

My dad, Danny and Ms. Kahn started to head down to Danny's new classroom while my mom and grandmother took their time saying goodbye to Lindsey. When they got down to Danny's classroom, all of the kids seemed eager to meet my brother. They couldn't believe how big he was. They were asking him questions about what sports he plays and what his favorite teams were. My brother seemed okay. He turned to my parents and grandmother and said "I'll be okay, you can go now." So, they said their goodbyes and left. They decided to head back toward Lindsey's class to take a peek in the window of the door to see if she was okay. Everything seemed fine for now, so they left.

In Jamie's Words

The bus pulled up and Lindsey got off first. She hopped off the stairs while holding hands with the girl that they paired her up with in class. They were both very excited. Boy, were we happy! It was definitely a change from that morning. My brother got off next, he just seemed okay. When we got inside we all wanted to know how their day was. Danny said it was good. He said he made some friends, but he missed his other friends. Lindsey said that she made a lot of friends, but she was missing her friends from the other school. We figured that it would take time before they both adjusted to the new school. I just felt really bad for my sister because it was her first experience with school other than preschool. I felt like it started off on the wrong foot for her and I was worried that it would leave a bad taste in her mouth for school in general. As far as my brother went, I was extremely concerned for him because my mom tried to have him moved in the beginning of the year, and the district said no. Now that they moved him in the middle of the year I really didn't know how it was going to affect him. My parents were just as concerned as I was. They didn't know how all of this was going to play out for him.

After their first day of school, my dad took them to the pediatrician's office to get checked because of the principal's assault. My dad really wanted to take them, instead of my mom, because he wanted to show the doctor what happened to his face as a result of all the stress. The doctor looked at Danny's arm and immediately saw the bruises. She couldn't believe it. She asked my brother to explain exactly what happened and he did. Then she looked at my sister's shoulders and saw that they still were sore to the touch. The doctor also asked my sister to explain what happened and she did. The whole time I think that the doctor was in total disbelief! *As a matter of fact, everyone we tell our story to is in total disbelief!*

A few days later the police officer called regarding the statement from the bus driver. She went on to say that she knew she wasn't being truthful because she had made references to keeping her job. The officer kept telling her that she wouldn't lose her job,

In Jamie's Words

that they wanted to arrest the principal but needed her statement as a non-biased witness to do so. The officer told us that there was nothing she could do for us unless the bus driver told the truth. Now I'm not a cop, but I'm certainly not stupid! How could there be no other way to make the arrest? She had 3 witnesses, 2 of them were victims. I think that the police department really needed to be held responsible for this because they left my family with no options and no recourse. My mom and dad kept going down to the precinct to try to get the police to make the arrest, but they still said no. They kept saying that they needed a witness who wasn't related to us. The part that I don't understand is if they knew that the bus driver was lying, why couldn't they arrest her for making a false statement? **Hopefully all of this will come out in court, and when it does, maybe we'll finally get the justice that's been long overdue!** In the mean time, my brother and sister were in the new school trying to make new friends and put the past behind them for now. Everything seemed fine until April 15th. My brother was on the lunch line outside the cafeteria in the hallway talking and laughing with friends. I think that he was finally feeling comfortable with the new kids and the new school so he let his guard down. **All of a sudden, an older woman came up behind him and dug her fingernails into his shoulder and then slammed him into the wall right behind him. The whole time this was going on, all the other kids on the lunch line saw what happened.**

Danny was startled and visibly upset. As he turned around to see her face he realized it was Ms. Gertrude from his prior elementary school. He told her to get her hands off of him and leave him alone. She continued to dig her nails into his shoulder while she pointed her finger in his face and told him to be quiet! Finally, she let go and walked away. All the kids on the lunch line asked Danny if he knew her and he said yes. My brother knew her from the other elementary school that he transferred from. Mrs. Gertrude was known at the other school for **SMOKING IN THE CLASSROOM!** She was also known for **HATING ALL OF THE BOYS AND GETTING PHYSICAL WITH THEM!** When I say physical, I mean grabbing their arm and twisting it or picking them up by their backpack and pushing them! What I'm getting at is that the other elementary school was complete chaos. Ms. Van Dyke was letting the teachers basically do whatever they wanted to whomever they wanted! So who knows what else happened there after my brother and I left?

I think that Mrs. Gertrude was pulled off of teaching because of her behavior and put into the other school to maybe learn a lesson. Needless to say, whatever the reason was she still got physically abusive with my brother!

When my brother got home, my dad took a look at his shoulder and you could still see the finger nail marks. Danny called my mom at the deli and told her what happened. ***My mother was so angry she could have spit fire!*** She was in total shock! She knew Mrs. Gertrude from the other school as well as knowing her reputation. She couldn't believe that she was in the other school with Danny and that she put her hands on him. My mom spoke with my dad and asked him to please try to call the district office while she called the principal. My mom tried several times to speak with the principal, but he was in a meeting and told his secretary that he would return the call when he was done. My dad got absolutely nowhere with the district. Mr. Butterman wasn't in so he left a message. My mom was frustrated because she couldn't get the principal. My brother had an ice pack on his shoulder to try to help with the marks and I was in total disbelief! Finally, my dad called the school back and spoke to the principal who said that he would get right on it. Apparently he called the district office and got a hold of Ms. Kahn for us and explained the situation to her.

The next morning, at 8:30am, Ms. Kahn called the house and spoke to my dad. She said that she was going to set up a meeting at the school with herself, my parents, my brother, the principal and Mrs. Gertrude.

The following week the principal called my house and spoke with my dad about coming in for that meeting. My parents agreed and went right in. When they got there, they called my brother down to sit with them before Mrs. Gertrude came in. My brother told the principal all about Mrs. Gertrude's reputation and how she was really mean to all of the kids. Apparently I was right in my theory about her being pulled off of teaching due to her disgusting behavior. The principal told them that she was a floater and was only allowed to help out at that school a few times a week.

They called Mrs. Gertrude in and she said hello to everyone in the room and sat down next to the principal. It was very difficult for my parents to stay calm and not choke her! She apologized to Danny for putting her hands on him, but she maintained the fact that she didn't hurt him. She said that she just tapped him. Now, my mom called some of the kids that were on that lunch line to ask them what they saw and they all told her that Mrs. Gertrude wasn't being gentle when she grabbed Danny. They told my mom that they couldn't believe what she did to him!

After that meeting was over, my parents spoke with the principal who really didn't know what to say to us. He obviously felt really bad about what happened. He kept saying that he was so sorry! My mom asked if Mrs. Gertrude could be removed from the school. The principal said that he would ask the district to remove

In Jamie's Words

her, but for now he agreed to take her off of lunch duty and keep her away from my brother. I felt so bad for my brother. I couldn't believe what was happening. As if all of the nonsense that Ms. Van Dyke caused wasn't enough! My brother took a spiral downward after that. He went into a deep depression and was always upset and didn't want to go to school. Aside from that, he felt very much alone. He wasn't happy doing anything. My parents tried so hard to do things with him to cheer him up but nothing was working.

Don't forget, my father still had Bell's palsy and was finding it very difficult to function, let alone go outside and try to live a normal life. My father was suffering from depression also due to his condition!

Right after this incident, my mom decided to close the deli. She couldn't handle any more stress. I was starting to get really nervous about my mother's health. All the hours she was working, all of the driving back and forth to Oyster Bay and all of the stress at home was really taking its toll. My mom was looking really tired and stressed. I saw that she wasn't feeling good most of the time.

Sometimes when she ate, the foods would make her sick. Little did we realize that she was becoming allergic to a lot of foods. All of a sudden she would eat something that had a seed or a pit in it and her throat would close. It would always happen if she made herself a peanut butter and jelly sandwich her throat would close. It turned out that she became allergic to **beans, nuts, seeds and pits.** I felt so bad for my mother. None of us knew what to do for her. She has been a really good sport about it and basically chalked her allergies up to stress! She kept saying that maybe one day when all the dust settles she'll be able to enjoy those foods again, but for now she struggled every day with allergic reactions with certain foods.

My mom had had a few interested buyers in the deli, but she couldn't wait that long. She papered the windows and let the staff go and handed the keys over to the landlord with all of the contents still left inside the deli and told the landlord to work it out. My mother really didn't want the deli anymore after my grandfather died. It was becoming a big burden. She was finding it hard to focus on business when she felt like the whole world was crumbling down around her.

In Jamie's Words

Personally, I think that she did the best thing because I felt like she was spinning her wheels and I wasn't sure where she would end up.

Without driving back and forth to Oyster Bay my mom was able to put things in perspective. It was at that time that I started to sit with her and do my timelines with all the dates and events that had taken place in the schools. My mom was also able to get my brother into therapy so he could try to work through his depression. My mom could not have done this if she still had the deli.

My mom was still tying up loose ends with the deli, while going to the district office to try to get Mrs. Gertrude removed, as well as helping my dad with his Bell's palsy. *I don't know how she did it! She was like super woman! How did she not crack? How did she manage to stay so focused and determined to win the fight? Honestly, how many fires was she trying to put out at the same time because it seemed as if there were many burning out of control all at once!*

My mom kept going up to the elementary school to speak with the principal to try to set up counseling for my brother with the

In Jamie's Words

school psychologist on a weekly basis. He had no problem with that. I think that he was still so bothered by what happened that he was willing to try anything to fix it.

So my brother would meet with the school psychologist to discuss his feelings and insecurities and she would try to reassure him. I don't know how much that was working, but my mom didn't give up. We all entered group therapy where we would meet once a week and sit with two therapists and discuss things for about an hour. It was working pretty well for a little while until we started to see that my brother was getting uptight with the whole thing. At that point we decided to split up the session time. My sister was being seen in one room, while my brother was being seen in another room. I would only go in when it was time for group therapy. I think that the therapists saw that my brother was more in need at that time than me. I was okay with that because I was very worried about my brother as well. It went well for a while. My brother's therapist was very patient with him even though she saw his state of mind. She

In Jamie's Words

also saw how loving and caring my parents were. That in itself was

a blessing even though my brother didn't see it that way.

I think my brother was putting a lot of blame on my parents

as if they didn't do enough for him and maybe they did more for me.

Even though this wasn't true, my parents decided to give Danny a

lot of one on one time. My dad would take my brother fishing,

sometimes at a local lake or on a big fishing boat. Other times he

would take him out to lunch or to a movie. Sometimes they would

go on a bike ride together or throw the football around in the yard.

As sick as my dad was he was willing to show my brother that he

was there for him.

My mother, also trying, would ask him what he wanted for

dinner and make his favorites. She and Danny would take the dog

for long walks together. They also decided to decorate Danny's wall

with a skateboard shelf and skating stickers. My mom tried really

hard to do creative things with him as well as spend quality time

with him. It wasn't easy! I don't know how they did it. I was getting tired just watching, but I knew that they loved him so much and were willing to do anything to make him whole again!

The therapist that was working with my sister was really great. You could tell that she really liked Lindsey and she saw my sister's potential. Lindsey was also showing signs of stress that's why my parents put her into a program as well. They felt that the extra attention to my brother may backfire and result in Lindsey feeling left out so they decided that this program would benefit her. Personally, I think that they did the right thing! Lindsey is a really great little girl with lots of love in her heart. I think that in time all of this will be behind us and all of our true colors will shine!

As for the rest of these idiots, one day they will get theirs! Hopefully, when that day comes they won't have the support of a loving family like me and my brother and sister have. Perhaps, they too will find themselves alone not knowing which way to turn or what to do. I don't wish this on them, but in life you have to be careful what you do, because it may all come back to haunt you one day!

CHAPTER EIGHT

7th GRADE "DEFAME"

I had a really great summer. My dad's Bell's palsy was improving. His face looked so good that it was hard for people to tell that he even had it even though he still had some symptoms. I spent a lot of time with some of my friends. I went to horseback riding camp and did a lot of fun day trips and activities with my family. I was in the play AIDA at The Airport Play House, which I was very excited about. This was the first non-school production that I was in.

In Jamie's Words

Everything seemed to be pretty good when school started. I had a lot of friends in my classes. Plus, I liked all of my teachers, and my teachers really liked me. I signed up for Art Club with Mr. Howard as the teacher. I was looking forward to it because Mr. Howard really liked me and saw my potential as an artist. I had high hopes that this year would be a great one for me. I felt as though things were moving in the right direction. I felt good about myself and my keeping my grades up. All I could do is hope for the best.

I signed up to be in the school play Joseph and the Technicolor Dream Coat, as well as Peter Pan at The Airport Play House, which was not a school production. I was excited about being in these two plays because I had hopes of getting a really good part. I've always dreamed of being an actress!

5th grade was good for my brother with no problems except for the fact that the bus driver who refused to tell the truth to the police about what she had witnessed was now the bus driver at my brother's new school. He was walking down the sidewalk heading toward the school when he heard someone calling him. He turned

In Jamie's Words

and saw her. She said hello to him and he said "What are you doing here?" She said "I really couldn't take it anymore at the other school; the principal is out of her mind!" My brother responded …well if it wasn't for you, I wouldn't have had to change schools because the principal would have been arrested! The bus driver tried every day to say hello to him, but my brother ignored her. I felt so bad for him because he had to see her every day. Whether he spoke to her or not didn't matter because he still saw her bus and it was an unpleasant reminder of what had happened in the other elementary school! As for my mom, she was just as angry to see her face there as well as the bus.

Life was going pretty well until I tried out for "Middle School Idol" in November '08, and made it into the first round. Of course, this gave all of the bullies a reason to pick on me more, as if they haven't done it enough. All hell broke loose because they were angry I made it. Even though some of them got picked also, they were still annoyed that I was now part of the "competition." But the whole idol thing was just for fun, almost like a talent show, but set up like "American Idol." From this moment on, nothing was the same. You might think that they would be happy for me, but NOOO! They were too consumed with their own lives, too consumed with hurting me! They kept asking me what song I wanted to sing in the first round, so I told them I wanted to sing "Get Back" by Demi Lovato. When it came time for telling the people who ran the program the 3 songs I wanted the most ("Get Back" by Demi Lovato, "Something I Don't Know" or "Keep Your Mind Wide Open" by Anna Sophia Robb), the bullies told me that that's the song they wanted, "Get Back", and that they had chosen that song before I thought of it. So, now you're going to argue with me over the song I chose? I figured that the idol staff would decide what song was best.

Just then, Nathaniel started calling me names. He sent me an Instant Message saying "YOU'RE THE BIGGEST B***H ALIVE!" Then he went on to call me a "WHORE", only he spelt it like "HO." He then tried to make it look like he was wishing me a "Merry Christmas." You know, "HO, HO, HO!" Can you imagine?

In Jamie's Words

Why did I have to endure more verbal abuse just because I was in the same competition as them? What kind of a SISSY picks on a girl anyway? I wasn't even letting him get away with it; I was giving it right back to him but he still continued! So, how many bully-free months did I have? Let's see…it was December now, so about 3 months. To think that I started this year with such enthusiasm and hope! Now I was back where it began. The only difference is that this time, the bullying consisted of one of the original bullies, who managed to **poison** my new friends. How does this happen? Why does this happen to ME?

I decided to drop out of the school play because all of the bullies knew that I signed up so they signed to bother me. This made me very upset because I was really looking forward to being in the show. I couldn't believe that they went ahead and signed up for stage crew, when they knew how passionate I was about being part of this production! I was so disappointed that I wound up dropping out of the play at The Airport Play House. I know that I probably

In Jamie's Words

shouldn't have let this get the best of me and drop out, but at that time I felt like it was the right thing to do.

In life, there are kids with all kinds of strange problems and terrible life styles, but they are left alone. Instead, they bother me, the one who concentrates, the one who has a stable life. Did these kids ever stop and look at themselves and notice what they have done to me? Or, take a good look at themselves and see what was wrong with them? I don't get it.

I decided that I was going to go to the 6th grade guidance counselor about Nathanial's Instant Messages in hopes that she would say something to him about his behavior, or maybe prevent him from participating in Middle School Idol. The reason I went to that counselor instead of the 7th grade one was because we had a history together and she knew the background of all of the bullying so I felt secure in confiding in her. Well, Mrs. Thompson called Nathaniel down to her office and explained to him that what he did was wrong and that he needed to apologize to me, otherwise he would not be able to compete. So, Nathaniel said he was sorry. It

In Jamie's Words

would have been nice if he meant it, because things only got worse after that. Maybe if there was a consequence, things would have gone differently. Now every time Nathaniel and his friend, Bradley, would pass me in the hall they would say "HO, HO, HO." I guess they figured they would get away with it because it was very close to Christmas. I don't get it. I didn't do anything to them. Why should I bother to go back to guidance and tell Mrs. Thompson, it wouldn't make it better!

Anyway, January 30th was here and I was very uptight about performing. To think that this should have been a very exciting and rewarding time in my life, but instead it was nothing but chaos. My mom helped me get ready and off to school we went. I wore a grey and white flowered tank top, skinny jeans with a zipper on both sides of the pant leg, a black blazer, and a cheetah print scarf. I had total self confidence for now, but didn't know what to expect when I got on stage.

Soon after my family sat down they realized that they were sitting just a few rows behind Jean, Dylan, Dana and Tess. I came out to see where my family was sitting and I saw the girls. Tess was the mutual friend of me and the girls; I was friends with her since 4th grade. I had a feeling that eventually Tess would soon have to choose me or them. Tess came right over to me as soon as she saw me and wished me luck, while the other girls turned and gave me dirty looks and called me names. At that moment all I could think of was what Mr. Jones had told my mom- "Bullies are too weak to act alone. They need others around them to feel strong and adequate!" Even though I knew that Mr. Jones was right, I was still yearning for my friends back. Tess walked away and sat back down with them. I felt really sad inside because I knew that my friendship with her was going to end after that night. I thought that maybe she would've stuck up for me and told Jean, Dylan and Dana to stop cursing me for no reason, but she didn't. She actually sat back down, turned her head and looked at me and laughed! It was almost as if the girls put her up to it, maybe to try to make me look like a fool or something. My family sat and watched the whole thing. My mom didn't get

In Jamie's Words

involved because her gut was telling her that there was more to come and her gut was right!

I left my family and went back behind the stage filled with pain and hurt inside. I didn't need this stress before I preformed. I really didn't want to go on stage. Do I call it quits and give them what they wanted, or do I give it my best shot and go out there and perform? Honestly, the last thing I wanted was to give any of these bullies the satisfaction of getting the best of me, but at the same token I truly wasn't in the right frame of mind to go on stage. What I didn't realize was that my family was watching all the things that the girls were doing. My grandmother couldn't believe the way they were behaving. They kept turning around and giving my family dirty looks. These girls have no respect. I would never be rude or disrespectful to someone's mom, dad or grandmother.

Soon, they announced my name to perform. I came out on stage and started to sing. I was so nervous and upset because of what was going on, but I did my best. My brother was taking lots of pictures of me while my mom was videotaping. I could hear my mom and family cheering for me along with lots of others, but the more my mom cheered, the more Jean, Dylan, Dana and Tess laughed. I was glad that my turn was over because it was no picnic backstage with the other bullies either! Normally, I would have no problem going out on stage and putting on a show, but these circumstances were different. So, not only did I have problems with the girls out front, but I had more comments and issues with Nathaniel and Margaret back stage. I was the 10th person to go on, and Margaret and Nathaniel were one of the last people to perform. There were a good 400 to 500 people in the crowd, but by the time they got to hear the last performers they were pretty "idoled" out!

I went running back to my family who greeted me with open arms, while Jean, Dylan and Dana turned around, looked at me and called me a "B****" really loud! Then, Tess got up and came over to me and told me that I did really well. She said that she made me a sign to cheer me on but she forgot it at home. Yeah, right! You remembered the sign for Nathaniel, but you conveniently forgot mine? The truth is, the girls told her that if she made me a sign that

In Jamie's Words

they would never speak to her again! This was told to me the next day in school! How two-faced could they be? Why am I a "B****?" Was it because I tried out and made it? Or, was it because they saw how supportive my family was? Or, maybe my presence around them was too much for them to handle. Maybe my sense of security and stability rubbed them the wrong way.

I was really annoyed that they were calling me a "B****". So was my mom. She got up, and looked for the guidance counselor Mrs. Thompson and when she found her she told her what was going on. Mrs. Thompson immediately went over to the girls and asked them to step outside in the lobby area. Dylan admitted to calling me a "B****" along with other names. Mrs. Thompson told them that they had to stop insulting me and that she would speak to them again the next day. The three girls walked back in and sat down. Tess came over to me and asked me why I got Jean, Dylan and Dana in trouble? Let's be real Tess! Did you not just see what was going on, or did you choose to look the other way? Then Tess walked away from me and sat down. I was FUMING! I could feel

In Jamie's Words

the heat coming off my body. Just then, Dylan texted me on my phone. She said "I'M REALLY SORRY! SOMETIMES I CAN BE REALLY SARCASTIC AND IF YOU NEVER WANT TO TALK TO ME AGAIN-THAT'S OKAY!" I saved the text message along with all of the other e-mails and I.M.s.

When it came time to choose who would move on to the next round in "Middle School Idol", I knew that I wouldn't! They brought everyone back onto the stage and then picked which ones were moving up. I wasn't one of those picked, but that's okay. I got up there and did the best I could under the circumstances. My family and I are very proud of that.

My mom always says that she doesn't know how I found the courage and strength to go onstage and sing. My family and I were getting ready to leave the auditorium when Dana came over to me and said "WHY THE HELL DID YOU DO THAT TO DYLAN?" "SHE DIDN"T DO ANYTHING TO YOU! WHAT THE HELL IS WRONG WITH YOU?" The next day, Mrs. Thompson called me down to her office to discuss how Dylan behaved last night. I told

177

In Jamie's Words

Mrs. Thompson about the text message and about what Dana said to me at the end of the night. We discussed lots of scenarios. Then she said that she would speak with Dylan and see if things could get better. Honestly, I wasn't so sure that I wanted things to get better. I didn't trust her or those girls. I mean really, what was she going to do? Say she's sorry and then go back to Jean, Dana and Tess and stab me in the back? The next day, Mrs. Thompson called me and Dylan down to her office. Dylan said again that she was sorry and that she understood if I didn't want to be friends anymore. I told her that I had no problem saying hi and bye in the hallway but I was going to PROCEED WITH CAUTION!

Two days later, In Tech class, I was working on a magnetic levitation car along with everyone else in the class. I had painted and decorated it. I was excited to finish this car because it was the first project that I had ever done by myself! Unfortunately, when I got to class, my car had been STOLEN out of Mr. Barilla's cabinet. All of the other cars were there except mine. Mr. Barilla looked everywhere with me to try to find it, but it was gone! I reported this incident to guidance as well as the assistant principal and principal.

Ms. Piper. What do you think they did? If you guessed NOTHING,

then you're correct!

The next day right after Jean and Dylan had Mr. Barilla for

their tech class, my car magically appeared upside down stuck in

one of the shelves, but the motor was missing. Mr. Barilla told me

not to worry, that he would order me another motor or get me one

from another school. So, lets' get this straight; everyone would

rather have me miss a full day of Tech class because I was looking

for my stolen project than find out who did this to me? Or better yet,

the school would rather go through the trouble of trying to find me

another motor for my car while I miss more of my Tech class

waiting for it to arrive, than find the kids that did this to me? IS

THIS A SCHOOL OR A CIRCUS? I know I've said this before but

it's true! I guess in this school I will always remain the VICTIM! No

one was willing to take a stand and fight for me. How sad! You see,

its behavior like this that made the bullying continue. Why would

the bullies stop now? They have it made! I mean, if you could steal

In Jamie's Words

someone's things out of a teacher's cabinet and get away with it, then why stop now!

This whole thing was just another disappointment to me and my family. What if it were the principal's things that were stolen-would there be consequences then? Would they view cameras and see who did it or would they just let it go and try to replace the items that were taken? Once again, I felt like I had no voice, that I wasn't heard! How could Mr. Morani and Ms. Piper just DISMISS ME like nothing mattered? Now my favorite class had become a nightmare! I FELT SO BETRAYED! My own classmates were all talking about it. They were all asking each other if they knew who stole my stuff. Before you knew it, they were all asking questions about the girls that I had been arguing with. Even my friend Isabella told me that she heard Jean and Dylan talking about how I must be on CRACK for thinking that it might be them who stole my project! Now I felt like my life was an open book. Everyone wanted to know my life. Nothing was private anymore.

In Jamie's Words

I couldn't understand how Mr. Barilla didn't demand to find out who did this to me. I mean, couldn't he have a STERNER talk with all of his classes and find out who stole my car and motor? Isn't this compared to an exam? If you steal it, you get suspended or better yet expelled. I truly felt so violated! I had to come to terms with this. I was realizing that this school really didn't care what happened to me!

Over the next two weeks, on a daily basis my hall locker was broken into. All of my Jonas Brothers pictures were taken. These were pictures that I took at their "Burnin' Up" concert along with pictures that I had cut out from the color booklet that I purchased at the concert. I also had other items in the locker that were tampered with like my favorite pink Hollister Sweater. The sweater looked like it had been taken out of my locker, stepped on a few times, scribbled on in pen and then put back. I went to speak to Mr. Morani on a daily basis about my locker. I asked him to please view the video cameras to see who did this to me- but he said NO! How could he choose not to view the cameras to see who was vandalizing my locker? I kept trying to tell him that I couldn't take it anymore! I was completely fed up with the school and the way they were doing things. I was tired of hearing that they didn't have enough time in their day to view the cameras or that my parents and I couldn't view them because it would violate privacy laws. What privacy laws? I have rights too! Didn't my rights mean anything? I GUESS NOT!

After two weeks of begging him to watch the videos and my parents going to the school and the district office, Mr. Morani decided that the solution would be to just give me a new lock! That's right, don't find out who stole my things, just let them keep doing it, just like the project in Mr. Barilla's class. What were these kids going to do next? That's what my family and I were afraid of! Once again I had no voice. The only people that cared were my family. Kids at school were all laughing as I would go by. It was becoming such a joke. Were my parents going to work so that they could replace what was being stolen? It sure seems that way!

MY PARENTS WERE FURIOUS! After filling out several complaint forms at the district office and having a meeting with Mr.

Morani and Ms. Piper, it left them unsatisfied. They decided to make another trip to the police department. I went with them. The police didn't have too much to offer us either. They told us that the situation had to be dealt with in the school because the kids were minors. I DON"T GET IT! IF THE MINORS KILLED ME WOULD THAT BE OKAY, TOO?

If the police had done their job, could they have prevented these kids from possibly growing up and becoming criminals! So let's think about this. The assistant principal doesn't want to exert himself to help me. He doesn't care if my personal belongings get stolen or not. The principal doesn't care either. The police don't care. What was I going to do? EVEN THOUGH I HAD MY FAMILY, I STILL FELT EXTREMELY ALONE!

My parents had many discussions with our attorney, Mitch Carlinsky, and my advocate and decided that another lawsuit would have to be filed. There was truly no other way to give me and my family the satisfaction that we wanted and so desperately deserved! Mitch Carlinsky also advised me and my family that from this point

In Jamie's Words

on, all conversations with the school had to be tape recorded. If the faculty and the school weren't going to protect me, then I had to protect myself! Each day that went by seemed like the only kids the school cared about were the bullies. I don't know what bothered us more, the fact that the school wasn't willing to give me the education that I deserved, or the fact that even the police didn't care enough about my well being.

On February 11th, I was at my lunch table where I had been sitting since September with Jean, Dana, Tess and Margaret and of course the girls were abusing me. I had tried to switch lunch tables while all of this was going on, but it's not as easy as you think. You have to go through certain processes before your table or your seat can get changed. You can only imagine what I must have been feeling, eating my lunch with them. I thought by now I would have been at a different table, but I was still working on it. Each day that I sat there it was getting worse and worse. They all had so many nasty comments. Most of the time I would just ignore it, but other times it was very difficult. I started to bring in a book to read after I was finished with my lunch. That became difficult also. I think the fact that I was living and breathing bothered them! There was another girl Sophie at the lunch table who I was friendly with. So we decided to eat our lunch real fast and leave the cafeteria and go to Mr. Barilla's class to finish our projects. The sad thing was that Sophie was a witness to all of the abuse that happened at the lunch table, but she wouldn't agree to go to guidance or the principal's office to help me get these girls punished! She would tell me that it didn't matter what they did even when they questioned why she was friends with me. She said that she was afraid of telling on them because she didn't want to go through what I was going through. I couldn't understand why she wouldn't want to help me. I was really hurt that she wouldn't come through for me. If the tables had been turned, I would have helped her because I believe in doing the right thing! If more people believed in that, the world would be a better place!

I was afraid of losing another friend, so I didn't let Sophie know how hurt I was. I was starting to feel like I was the

MINORITY, like there was something wrong with me. I took a good look at myself and analyzed everything that was going on and really didn't think that I was at fault! I felt strongly that if the school would have made some phone calls home to the parents of these girls, things may have been different. Who knows what they were going home and telling their parents. They could have gone home and told them that it was me doing all these terrible things to them. If the school would have taken a stand to defend me and punish these girls, or made some phone calls home, I think that their parents may have viewed what they were doing differently! Could it be that there weren't any more loving parents that care about what kind of trouble their kid is getting into? Was I really the minority because I came from a loving and caring home? Was there something wrong with my parents because they wanted this bullying nonsense to stop? Was there something wrong with my home life because my parents care who my friends were and cared about where I was?

What is this world coming too? How come no one wants to take a stand and stick up for someone else? What if it were Sophie who was being bullied? What if I had witnessed it and just let it go? That wouldn't be right. What if these girls did something really bad to Sophie and I could have done something to stop it and didn't. I would never be able to live with myself. Am I the only one left in the school that truly cares about others? It most certainly looks that way! Anyway, as soon as lunch was over I went to my next class only to hear that Nathaniel and Bradley were going around school telling everyone that "JAMIE SUES ALL THE KIDS AND THEIR FAMILIES THAT BOTHER HER!" I needed this? I was furious! I went down to Mr. Morani's office and told him what was said. He told me that he would call Bradley down and speak to him and that he would allow me to change tables for lunch. I was a little unsure if I wanted to do that. I told him that I would take a good look around the cafeteria tomorrow and see where else I could sit. I was also afraid that things may get worse if I moved. I was unsure of how it would pan out. In my mind I felt like if I moved that the bullies won! The last thing I wanted was to give the bullies any satisfaction.

In Jamie's Words

As far as Bradley went, I think that after Mr. Morani called him down to the office, he called his mother and discussed it with her. The only reason that I think that happened was because as soon as I got home that day I got an I.M. from another so-called friend Claire. She went on to tell me that Bradley was really upset in the middle of the day because of something that I did and that I made him cry! I told her that it was something that he did, not what I did. I told her exactly what happened and she still got nasty with me and said how dare I hurt him like that! So I'm thinking to myself and saying "I hurt him?" I couldn't believe it. I thought for sure that when Claire heard what was going on, she would be more sensitive to my situation, but I was very wrong!

I guess I lost another friend. I kept telling myself that girls like this weren't worthy of my friendship, but in the mean time I was really hurting. My parents tried to tell me that I was so much more mature than all of these kids and that one day I would finally meet some true friends. Even though that sounded pretty promising it really wasn't making me feel better now! The next day, February

In Jamie's Words

12th, I was harassed in lunch again. This time Margaret started in about my dad. She said how I idolized him and how she was sick of hearing how wonderful he was. That's because her dad wasn't around. Once again, this is an example of a kid being jealous of the fact that I had a stable life! It also rubbed her the wrong way because my dad has met a lot of famous people in his life time, a lot of them that he keeps in contact with. I told Margaret that my dad is a really great guy and it's too bad if it rubs you the wrong way! Well, that started another World War!

In the mean time, I was trying to look around the cafeteria to see where I could sit and it wasn't looking good. In one corner you had the girl from 5th grade Philomena that wanted to "KILL THE RAT" (the rat was me). In the other corner you had the girl Josephine who bothered me in 5th grade, whose father and brother supposedly deal heroin out of their home. I was already having problems with Josephine again. She was starting to chime in and instigate a lot of the bullying. I really didn't know what I was going to do. I had nowhere to sit except with the bullies. Now I had

In Jamie's Words

Margaret making nasty comments about my dad. I was really getting

uptight. What I wanted to do was SCREAM at the top of my lungs

and tell everyone to go to HELL!"

Of course Sophie didn't want to get involved in this one

either. How could she just sit there and not open her mouth? She

walked out of the cafeteria with me and told me how much she hated

Margaret. She just kept saying that Margaret is BIPOLAR! She went

on to tell me about all of her mood swings. Personally, I didn't care

about her mood swings. I had enough on my plate. Honestly, I didn't

know how I sat at that table for as long as I did. When I think back I

think that the only reason I sat there was to prove a point. In my

mind, I proved to myself that I wasn't so fragile and that I wouldn't

break so easily!

On February 23rd '09, my mom and dad decided to go to

school again to speak with Mr. Morani and Ms. Piper as well as the

guidance counselor Mr. Bumble who supposedly specialized in

bullying. Well, that was a JOKE! Mr. Bumble had agreed to see me

a few times a week to help me with answering these bullies, but all he ever did was give me a sheet on what to say to someone if they didn't like my shirt. I wish that's all these bullies didn't like about me because that would have been really easy to fix!

My parents asked why the other girls couldn't move from the table, why it had to be me. They said that it would just be easier to move me instead of all the girls that were bothering me. Ms. Piper even had the nerve to tell my parents that "THERE WERE TOO MANY KIDS INVOLVED TO GET THIS TO STOP!" Well that's promising, don't you think? The principal of your middle school tells your parents that she basically can't protect you in this school! If she would have done her job in the first place there wouldn't be too many kids involved.

I was realistic and I knew that not every kid will like you. You have to expect some bumps in the road. Not every day can be filled with flowers and butterflies! Unfortunately, there haven't been any peaceful times or memorable times in this school or my elementary school. It's only been really upsetting and hurtful! To think that Ms. Piper and Mr. Morani were also holding the key to my freedom. How could they just continue to let these kids hurt me? Didn't they feel any remorse? I guess not! Maybe if it happened to their kid they would have felt differently! Maybe they should have been taught the right way to interrogate someone to get the truth out of them.

It's really sad that they, too, let me and my family down! They told my parents that they really didn't know what to do to catch these kids in the act. Give me a break! Do we have to do their job for them and put a stop to this bullying, because they sure don't know how to make it stop!

My parents felt as though they were banging their heads against the wall. *The school staff, as well as this so-called bully expert, Mr. Bumble, were a complete waste of our time!* My parents put me back into a therapy program that was geared toward my bullying needs. At least this way my parents felt that I would have someone else to talk to about this other than them. At first I really didn't want to go, but after going a few times it became easier and easier to talk with her and trust her. Needless to say, she couldn't believe what the school was allowing to take place. She agreed that this was an out of control situation that needed to stop! She feared for my safety also! The best part of seeing this therapist was that she was on my side and believed in me. She knew that it wasn't anything that I did to precipitate all of this bullying and harassment. Also, my family and I knew that after seeing her for a while that eventually she would testify for me in court. I was really happy about this. I FELT LIKE SHE HEARD MY VOICE!

Unfortunately, the situation at school was getting worse. The harassment went on at the lunch table for weeks as well as the bullying in all of my classes. The number of kids that were bullying me was growing and there were more boys chiming in each day! I was getting really tired of all of this and so were my parents. My parents started to look for private schools for me to attend. They searched on the web. They made lots of phone calls and lots of appointments, but ultimately we had chosen the one that I had always been impressed with! My parents took me to interview with the school and they liked me as much as I liked them. I think that they saw that I had a lot to offer them as well as what they had to offer me. I was thinking that maybe I would finally get the education I deserved! My mom took me to their open house where I got to tour the whole school and meet some of the staff and kids and I loved it even more. I felt really safe there. I felt like no one could ever hurt me again!

In the meantime, I was still stuck in this HELLHOLE of a school! My parents couldn't move me until seventh grade was over. This meant about four more months of torture!

On March 5th, Jean and Mary Jo flipped my lock in gym. All the school had to do was check the cameras by the gym to confirm who did it, but once again they wouldn't. My parents and I went to speak with Mr. Morani and Ms. Piper because Jean sent me a text message saying that it wasn't her that flipped my lock- that it was Mary Jo! I brought my cell phone with me to show them the text message so that Mary Jo would get in trouble but they refused to look at it. Instead they decided to move my locker in gym. *Once again I was the victim and the school was bowing down to the*

In Jamie's Words

bullies. I was made to look like a fool repeatedly at the hands of the school instead of them just doing their job and suspending these kids. Now I was made fun of again because it was my locker that had to get changed, not theirs. ***I was so disgusted with the system! How could they continue to allow these girls to try to destroy me?*** Ms. Piper and Mr. Morani spoke with the gym teacher, Ms. Riley, and asked her to keep an eye on things. My mom put a call into Ms. Riley because I had come home from school upset again about a situation in gym. She called my mom back and told her that she did see Jean and Mary Jo being really loud and obnoxious and how their behavior could intimidate someone. OKAY, so if you saw this firsthand, don't you think you should do something about it? Ms. Riley told my mom that she wasn't willing to report it back to Ms. Piper or Mr. Morani but once again she would continue to keep an eye out. Keep an eye out, for what? *Did she think that eventually she would find my dead, bloody body lying on the floor in the gym?* Maybe this is what the school and the district was waiting for. Maybe they thought that that was the way to get this to stop?

In Jamie's Words

Anyway, I don't know how good her eyes were because during gym, on March 9th, Jean and Mary Jo decided to take their cell phones out and take a picture of my birthday invitation which had my new home phone number on it. My parents felt it necessary to change the number because of all of the harassment. I put the new number on my birthday invitation because I was only giving it to a few girls, but I probably should have just put my cell number instead. I figured with my home number I wouldn't get any texts.

On March 10th, Jean, Tess, Dana and Margaret demanded that I throw their garbage away at the lunch table. I told them no! They started to call me "GARBAGE GIRL!" They kept telling me that it was my job to throw away their garbage because I had been helping Tess for a few weeks in school due to a fractured collarbone. I had no problem throwing away Tess's garbage when her arm was in a sling, but her arm was better. She just wanted to harass me and use me along with the other girls. Margaret kept telling me that I had to throw the garbage away because I was worthless. This made me very angry and what made it worse was that Sophie was just sitting there watching. When I finally got them to be quiet and stop abusing

me, Dana opened up her bag of chips and started throwing them at

me. I started yelling at Dana to stop throwing food, but it got me

nowhere, because they all started arguing who was going to throw

away the garbage. Sophie got up and threw away everyone's

garbage! I got up and ran after Sophie and said "WHAT THE HELL

ARE YOU DOING, YOU'RE NOT THEIR SLAVE, DON'T

TREAT THEM LIKE PRINCESSES!" Sophie said "WHATEVER,

I'M NOT GOING TO CAUSE A PROBLEM, I'M JUST GOING

TO DO WHAT THEY WANT AND THROW AWAY THEIR

GARBAGE!" I was really mad! Sophie had just shown me that she

was truly no better than them. In fact she was probably worse!

Anyone that can stand there and watch an innocent person get

tormented, abused and have food thrown at them was not worth my

time! At that point I got up and went to the office to speak with Ms.

Piper or Mr. Morani. Mr. Morani spoke with me briefly as I

explained what had just happened and how Sophie was my witness.

He decided not to call Sophie in to talk to her. Instead, he said that

In Jamie's Words

he would tell Mr. Barilla that I could still go to his class to hang out during lunch. Does this sound normal? You have all these witnesses that would probably tell the truth to Mr. Morani, especially if he asked the questions properly! Why wouldn't he want to stop the bullying? Didn't he realize that once they were finished with me they would move onto someone else? Did he not have the capacity to see what was really going on? Maybe the district should replace him with an assistant principal who knows how to do his or her job! On Monday, March 16th, I decided that I was going to change lunch tables. It wasn't about winning the fight any more. It was about keeping my sanity! I sat down at my new table with this girl that I had recently met, named Jordan. As soon as I got my lunch and sat back down, Margaret, Jean, and Dana came over to the lunch table to harass me. I told them to go back to their own table and leave me alone. Jordan was my witness to this abuse but no one seemed to care not even the lunch teachers on duty. Don't you think that the staff would want to put this behind them and just fix the problem?

In Jamie's Words

This bullying problem was becoming very tiresome! I didn't want to have to deal with these girls anymore at lunch, I didn't want to continue to go to my locker any more, I just wanted a new life! I started to carry all of my books in a book bag and a large binder. My back and shoulders were killing me, but it seemed to be the only way to protect my personal property. So basically I thought that I had solved the locker stealing issue and I thought that I solved the lunch table issue, but I was very, very wrong! The next day my dad went back to the school and spoke to Mr. Morani and told him that we were going to continue to go to the police regarding the thefts in my locker and all of the continued abuse that I had to endure on a daily basis. My dad told him that this school was completely out of control and that we weren't going to stop until we got justice for me! *Mr. Morani seemed very unconcerned! I think that he was finding all of this extremely amusing!* I'll tell you one person that wasn't laughing: Mr. Jones from *The Center for School Safety in Albany*! Mr. Jones had made several phone calls to the district regarding the treatment that I was experiencing. Occasionally, the district would listen to what he said, but for the most part they were trying to placate us and then would do nothing! The good thing is that Mr. Jones is a very knowledgeable man who is probably going to be deposed or testify for us, but the best thing about him is that he had a heart! He always cared about what happened to me and my family. He really couldn't believe how long this harassment was being allowed to go on for. There was no reason for it. It was almost like the school staff was getting off on it!

Two days later, I was sitting at the new lunch table when a boy named Clark stood up and yelled to everyone in the cafeteria, "Jamie sues everyone!" He made such a scene! Everyone in the cafeteria heard including the lunch teachers! I wanted to crack Clark across the face and drop a cement block on these girls' feet for instigating this! I couldn't believe that this kid was getting involved in a situation that he wasn't a part of.

First of all, I don't sue everyone. We only sued the district and named all teachers and principals that were a party to this harassment. But the middle school hadn't even been served yet with its lawsuit. Only the elementary school, had been served and the district. Now that I think about it, kids from the elementary school like Amelia and her friends must have been the ones that started that rumor about me suing everyone. So this kid took it upon himself to defame me to the whole cafeteria. There were so many witnesses! I ran to the office again and told Ms. Piper and Mr. Morani what happened. I gave him the name of the boy who did this to me and guess what happened next? Mr. Morani called the wrong Clark down to the office! **I wonder what kind of degree Mr. Morani has, because I think that he may have gotten it out of a Crackerjack box!**

Clark got up from his lunch table on March 19th and went over to the lunch line where I was standing and told everyone that I sue people that bother me. Then he got other kids involved to chime in and harass me. What I hadn't realized was that Margaret precipitated it. She had gone over to him and told him to do that. All the lunch teachers saw what happened. They went over to Clark and told him to sit down. After he sat down, he still continued to yell things at me. The lunch teachers ignored him after that, but everyone still heard him! You would think that the lunch teachers would go to the office and tell the principal what happened, but they didn't want to get involved in helping me either! I went back to the office and told Mr. Morani what happened and who the witnesses were. Mr. Morani again called the wrong Clark down to his office. All he had to do was speak with the witnesses, but that would have been too simple! **Here again Mr. Morani tried to make me look like a fool, but who was really the FOOL?** Later that day, I went to Mr. Barilla's class for Tech and once again MY PROJECT WAS STOLEN! This time Mr. Barilla took my project which was a metal box that was to become a desk organizer with my name carved into it and put it in a different cabinet in a different tech room. We looked everywhere for it. I was more upset than angry because it took me a long time to cut and spot weld it. We thought that it was put away safely. I guess not!

Mr. Barilla gave me some wood to start my desk organizer so that I could get busy on that while he looked for my metal box.

In Jamie's Words

What a disappointing day! First Clark made a scene in the cafeteria and now another project got stolen. I came home and told my parents. Of course they were very angry. They placed a call to Ms. Piper and Mr. Morani, but they had already gone for the day. The next morning my mom spoke with Mr. Morani. He said that he would look into the incident. YEAH, RIGHT! By now if I were the principal, I would have sat the whole 7th grade down and questioned or threatened them with suspension until someone came forward with my project. IT WAS AS IF I DIDN'T EXIST! No one in the school cared what was done to me and no one cared what was taken! This wasn't your typical teasing; this was becoming a very serious issue! I WAS STARTING TO FEEL INVISIBLE! Over the course of the next three days I carved my wood for my desk organizer while Mr. Barilla ordered me another piece of metal. I had already fallen behind because of the stolen metal box. The whole class was ahead of me.

I was so upset, I could hardly think straight! Once again, how could the school not watch the videos to see who was taking my things? **Didn't I matter? Everyone else was getting their education, what about me?** The next day I re-made my metal box. I engraved my name in it again only this time Mr. Barilla hid it behind his computer. I took the carved wood home with me. I figured that this was the only way to prevent someone from stealing it!

IT'S SO SAD ISN'T IT? I WAS SLIPPING THROUGH THE CRACKS! **I was so smart and creative, but I was worth nothing in this school!** My parents went to the district office and spoke to the assistant superintendent of the middle schools and requested 22 harassment complaint forms. He was reluctant to give them to my parents, but my mom demanded them! My parents discussed their disappointment in the school system and told him that we weren't going to back down until justice was served! When my parents got home they called Mr. Jones and told him what was going on. As usual, he was appalled at what the school district was allowing to happen. He suggested that it was time for me to find another school! My parents told him that they were going to move

In Jamie's Words

me to a different school at the end of the summer, but that wasn't stopping the bullying now! My mom then called my advocate and discussed the situation with him. He told my mom that the school had broken so many laws where we were concerned that it was ridiculous. He told my mom to go back to the library and photocopy the school laws that were violated. So my mom went and did more research and made more copies. She called my advocate back and went over some of the violated laws and they decided to just hold on to them for now as eventually they would be needed for court. I'm a human being with feelings and I didn't appreciate what was going on! I didn't know who I was angrier at -the bullies or the school!

If you think about it, the school was no better than the bully. They were breeding bullies therefore they were bullies themselves! A few days later, I was in homeroom in Ms. Rosario's class and Clark started in again. We were studying for a social studies test and I lent the teacher my notes when out of nowhere Clark said "EEWW, YOU'RE GONNA GET THE SUE ME COOTIES!" Ms. Rosario said "That's not nice Clark; Jamie was nice enough to give us her Social Studies notes so that all of you could pass your test."

Clark continued with his annoying behavior so Ms. Rosario had him

sit in the corner of the classroom for the rest of the class. What she

should have done was sent him down to Mr. Morani so that he could

get in trouble. But that would have been the right thing to do. Two

days later it was my 13th birthday. I didn't make a big deal at all. I

was just kind of hoping that I would get through the day without

issues. I kept to myself most of the day. Sophie went over to Tom,

the security guard, and asked him to sing Happy Birthday to me. So,

that's exactly what he did. He managed to get the whole cafeteria to

sing, except for Margaret, Jean, Dana, Clark, Tess, Josephine and,

Philomena. I was so happy that they were singing for me that I

really didn't notice some didn't sing for me. I saw Tess get up and

go over to the lunch table that Josephine and Clark were sitting at,

but I really didn't hear what she said. The bell rang. We got up and

left the cafeteria. My friend Luke came over to me and told me that

Tess came over to the table that he was sitting at with Clark and

Josephine. He said that Tess told them all not to sing for me because

In Jamie's Words

I didn't deserve it. Luke told her that that wasn't nice and that I was really a nice person. With that, I went to the office and spoke to Mr. Morani and brought him up to speed on what the bullies were doing during lunch. It wasn't that I didn't want to fight my own battles. I was just so disgusted with the whole situation that I wanted the office to know that even when I switched lunch tables it still wasn't stopping. I also knew that Luke was going to the principal's office also to tell them that he'd been witnessing the harassment all the time. Later that day, I met up with Luke who told me that he went down to the principals' offices to tell them about what was going on in the cafeteria and Mr. Morani yelled at him. He supposedly told him that he was the troublemaker and that if he didn't mind his own business that he would be punished! So let me spell this out for you. This means that witnesses were coming forward to defend me and try to get these kids punished for what they were doing and Mr. Morani and Ms. Piper didn't want to hear it! How disgusting is this! **How could they sit back and watch a child's life completely unravel? This proved to me and my family that they truly had**

no compassion for what was going on, nor did they care. Furthermore, they were getting a rise out of it!

My dad called Mr. Morani to discuss these issues, but nothing was ever done or addressed. The police department didn't want to hear it anymore and neither did the district. Shame on all of them! I had a voice that needed to be heard! How dare they deny me my Constitutional Rights? My family and I had done everything right! We took the legal route as opposed to the physical route like I'm sure many would have done by now! We tried extremely hard to keep our hands clean while getting the best professional help we could. How dare they try to repeatedly harm us! It was becoming like it was their mission to destroy us! It was like some kind of weird VENDETTA! About a week later, I was in Ms. Rosario class when Clark came in and immediately started in with me about the *"sue me cooties."* Ms. Rosario told him to stop but he continued. So for the whole class, I had to endure abusive behavior because Ms. Rosario didn't want to send him to the principal's office to get in trouble. Why was everyone completely numb to my situation? Were they just really stupid or were they somewhat inhuman? It definitely seemed that way! A few days later I was in my remedial math class. I had to take this class because I was failing math due to all of the bullying. Anyway, I was sitting there, minding my own business, when the teacher stepped out into the hallway to speak with another teacher. As soon as she stepped out, Jean and Mary Jo started to curse at me and roll up small pieces of paper and throw them at me. I kept telling them to stop but they were laughing and taunting me. Mary Jo started telling me how she hates horses and what an "***-hole" I was for having them. She went on to say that she was going to hurt me and my family and especially my horses. I tried to ignore her but I was very uptight. The next morning I went to the principal's office and asked Mr. Morani if I had to stay in the remedial math class any longer because I couldn't take it anymore. He asked why. I told him what was going on with Jean and Mary Jo and I told him that it really didn't matter anymore what they said to me or what they did because they had already done enough! He said that he would talk to Ms. Piper about moving me out of that class,

In Jamie's Words

but he wasn't sure. Two days later, I was back in my remedial math class. I had seen Mr. Morani speaking with the math teacher in the hallway prior to me going to that class. Here I was thinking that maybe he was speaking to her about my grades so that I could move out of the class, but instead he was talking with her to see if she had witnessed anything going on with Jean and Mary Jo. Honestly, don't you think by now he should have just taken my word for it? There were so many instances, why would you look to confirm another one? Just take my word for it! It was almost as if he was investigating me! I guess to him, I was the bad kid that kept complaining and all the other kids were just being kids, even if those other kids were extremely abusive and destructive. **When Ms. Bottomsly saw me coming into the room, she was very annoyed. She stood in the front of the classroom and yelled at me as all the kids were coming in. She accused me of involving her in my problems. She started screaming at me and saying that she didn't care what was going on with certain girls, in or out of her classroom! Then she started to separate all of the seats and split**

210

us up. She purposely surrounded me with the bullies. It was so intentional, I couldn't believe it! Meanwhile, everyone was looking at me. Some kids felt really bad for me, while the bullies all looked at each other and laughed and clapped. So now I was made to look like a fool in front of everyone by a teacher. Just great! I don't know how I stayed in that classroom for the rest of the period.

My mom was really upset with me for staying. She kept asking me why I didn't grab my things and walk out! I told her that I thought that I was in shock and for a little while I felt numb where I couldn't even feel my legs or feet. My mom wasn't angry at me, but she said that enough was enough and if that would've been her sitting there she probably would have had some choice words for the teacher even if it meant getting yelled at again, at least then there would have been a good reason to be yelled at! After class was over, a few of my friends came over to me and said "What was that all about?" I filled them in and they were very sorry for me. They told me that if I was going to tell the principal or the district about Ms. Bottomsly, they would gladly be my witnesses. I was happy for that.

211

At least I felt like I had a few people in my corner. My mom called the school to speak with the principal, but she was already gone. So on Monday, my parents went up to the school and had a meeting with Ms. Piper, Mr. Morani and Mr. Bumble. They explained what the teacher had done to try to embarrass and humiliate me in front of the bullies. Ms. Piper seemed confused as if she didn't quite understand what really took place. *Maybe she found it hard to believe that her teachers were dysfunctional too!*

They called me down to their office and I explained it to them. I told them that I had witnesses and they were willing to come down and tell them exactly what happened. My parents also told them that I was not going back into that classroom for remedial math and that they had better find another place for me to go during that period! I'm not sure if those witnesses were ever questioned and I don't know what happened to Ms. Bottomsly. I know that the next day she wasn't in school, I don't know if she was suspended for the day or out sick? Either way, they refused to tell my parents what her consequences were! The only good thing that came out of this was that the principal agreed that I shouldn't return to remedial math so she decided to give me a library period instead.

The next day my mom went to speak to the middle school superintendent. My mom was furious about what had taken place with the teacher and the girls involved. My mom made extra copies of harassment complaint forms so she had them to fill out. Prior to meeting with Mr. Babble, she filled out a whole bunch of them and brought them with her. My mom is a stickler for being organized and for making sure she left a paper trail of events! She gave Mr. Babble all the paperwork and asked him to please look into what happened to Ms. Bottomsly as a result of her actions. He said he would and then get back to her. Then he handed the complaint forms over to Miss Lasher, the compliance officer. Miss Lasher went over to my mom and told her that she only handles sexual harassment complaints, not regular complaints. My mom asked her who handles regular harassment complaints, she said "the principal." So basically, things just get passed off with no consequences for everyone but me! *If you think for one minute that Mr. Babble*

213

In Jamie's Words

actually did something human and decent and took care of my problem, you're wrong! He never even had the decency to call my mom back even after my mom had put several phone calls into him regarding this matter.

That afternoon, I received an I.M. from Jean. It said her screen name and that she was available. Then she said "whoz dis?" I answered her back and said "who is this?" Then she came back on and said "Jean, whoz dis?" Then it went on to say "dey ganna sing da F.U.N. song nd Striped Sweater Song even if I hve to pay dem! nd imma make sure Jaime wears his D**K hatt!" lmfaoooo Dylan!<3"

The next message came in a few minutes later and it said, "wait is dis Jamie?" I didn't answer her, even though I wanted to jump into the screen and strangle her! I tried to control myself and maintain my dignity. I told my parents what was going on and they agreed not to have me answer her. I saved the I.M.s and printed them out. At first I didn't know who it was because I switched my screen name to avoid being harassed and I blocked all of the bullies.

In Jamie's Words

They in turn changed their screen names so they could continue bothering me! You can tell just by reading it that Jean is totally illiterate and trashy. The next day I got the same rude I.M., but this time it was from Jean, Dylan and Clark. It said "**JAIME BEST WEAR HIS D**K HATT CUZ HE LOOKS AMAZZZINNGGGG IN ITTT!:) lmfaooo Dylan! Clark<3.** This is exactly how it was written. It came from Jean's computer and up at the top of the page it said her screen name and that she was mobile. I guess that once she saw that Ms. Bottomsly was abusing me, she figured that it was time to chime in! Hey let's face it, it was a free for all so why not right? The sad part is that Jean really needed more than just remedial math classes. From the looks of her grammar it appears that she needed remedial everything! That night my father took me to the police department and they issued me a central complaint number for the police report as well as telling me that it was an "Aggravated Harassment!" We were very happy with this. We had hoped that the next step would lead to their arrests! The next day I went to school and I was really keeping to myself. I was

In Jamie's Words

happy with the outcome so far with the police and I knew that my parents were coming up to speak with Ms. Piper and Mr. Morani about the Aggravated Harassment charge. I was just upset because of all of the turmoil; I felt like I was spinning my wheels as well. I had a lot of mixed emotions that day.

My parents had gone out to lunch to try to spend some quality time together and then they were going to come to the school. Unfortunately, I had to disturb their lunch with more bad news from school! I was sitting in my regular math class and Jean kept walking past me. I had my book bag next to my chair on the floor. Every time she walked past me she touched my book bag. I kept moving my chair a little to try to get away from her. First she went to the back of the room to use the pencil sharpener that she knew was broken. She walked past me and touched my bag and then headed up to the front of the class to use the pencil sharpener. Then she repeated that pattern again. When class was over, I picked up my book bag and put it on my shoulder. I headed out of the classroom when all of a sudden my shirt felt really wet on the side that my book bag was on. I went to my next class which was Tech.,

I put my bag down and liquid was pouring out of it. My whole side

was soaked. I started to empty my bag and everything inside my bag

was ruined! I was flipping out! Some of my friends in the class came

over to me to see what was wrong. They couldn't believe what all of

my things looked like. The most upsetting part was that I'm a huge

"Twilight" fan and I had one of the books with me because I read at

lunch. Well, my book was destroyed! It was soaking wet with the

cover starting to shred. I showed the teacher what everything looked

like and asked if I could please go to the office. He let me go and

that's when I called my parents. This whole ordeal with the liquid

that got poured into my bag took a matter of two minutes to happen.

Can you believe how a life can change in 1-2 minutes? I was so

upset. I couldn't believe that someone would stoop that low to try to

destroy my property like this. How could she do this to me? My

parents flew over to the school. When they got there, I was waiting

for them. My mother called security over in the office along with

some of the office staff. Mr. Morani had someone in his office, but

217

In Jamie's Words

he came out when he heard my mom yelling. My mom took everything out of my book bag while my dad was picking all of the wet items up and showing everyone. My father kept saying **"Enough is enough, when is this all going to stop!"** My mother took a look and said that it looked like blue Gatorade was poured in the bag because everything had a blue streak dripping off of it. My dad thought it looked water but when it was poured inside of the blue book bag the color of the bag must have run!

The whole time I was crying and listening to my mother say maybe it was Gatorade, maybe it was water. I heard Mr. Morani asking me who touched my bag. Everyone was talking and yelling at once! I couldn't believe that my textbooks, notebooks and "Twilight" book were garbage! I tried to pull myself together and tell Mr. Morani what happened in Math class with Jean walking past me and touching my bag. I never accused Jean for pouring a liquid into my bag because I never saw her put it in. It's just ironic that my book bag was dry up until the end of that class and then my bag was soaked. There's no explanation! Mr. Morani couldn't speak with us

218

In Jamie's Words

any longer because he did have someone waiting for him in his office. My mom handed him a copy of the police report regarding the I.M.s. My dad told him that he expected him to punish these kids for harassing me on a line. My mom explained to him that there were state laws that prohibit on and off campus bullying. They told him that they were formally withdrawing me from the school because it was completely out of control. My dad told Mr. Morani that he should be ashamed of himself for letting this carry on as long as it did. He then told him that one way or another we were going to get justice!

Afterwards, my mom and dad went to the district office and spoke to Mr. Butterman the superintendent. My dad told him about all of the instances that had taken place and what he was going to do about them. Mr. Butterman's comment was "This is very interesting; there is another family in one of our other schools that's having a similar problem. Maybe I should give you her information so you could compare?" **What the hell was that?** Was this some kind of a sick twisted joke? *Maybe we should have you arrested so you could*

compare notes with the other inmates! Then he went on to say that maybe I should wear a wire? Personally I haven't heard that term used in a long time, I think he was watching too many old FBI movies! I wish I had that kind of time on my hands, but I'm too busy fighting off bullies!

My dad gave Mr. Butterman a copy of the police report that said Aggravated Harassment. My parents also showed him a letter from my therapist suggesting homeschooling for the remainder of the month. He seemed very unconcerned. Of course he wasn't concerned, he's a MORON! He cared more about his hair and his suits than he cared about human life! My parents told him that they weren't 100% sure about homeschooling because once again it was another step that we as a family were taking to ensure my safety, not a measure that the school was taking to put a stop to these kids harassing me!

We taped this conversation as well, so if Mr. Butterman decides to read this he'll know that my parents took his advice and decided to wear a wire every time they spoke to him! The

next day I stayed home from school. It was the first absence that I had all year. Even with all of the bullying, I still took pride in my work and tried to remain a focused student. I had to stay home from school because I felt completely drained and depressed. I felt like I couldn't go any further. I did take a shower and get ready because my mom wanted to take me up to school to speak with Mr. Morani and Ms. Piper regarding the conversation with the police and their meeting with Mr. Butterman and also the outcome of the possible punishment of the bullies who were IMing me nasty things! My mom and I went up to the middle school later that morning. As soon as we walked in I saw my friend Jordan sitting at our lunch table. She immediately called me over to find out what was going on and why I wasn't in school. I told her briefly what was going on and she told me that Mr. Morani called everyone down to his office to question them about the water damage in my book bag. She told me that she told Mr. Morani that she saw Jean with a water bottle in that class but she didn't see her pour anything into my bag. Well, that was good enough for me. I felt like I had a witness that at least saw

In Jamie's Words

something positive in my defense. Mr. Morani saw me speaking with Jordan so he came over to the table and asked me to step out into the hall and speak with him. Everyone was very confused. They didn't know what happened. They thought that I was suspended! I was walking back to the main office with my mom and Mr. Morani. He wasn't sure if I was actually in school that day. I told him that I came back up to school to find out the outcome of my damaged items and to get my wet book bag back! He asked my mom and me if we would step into his office and speak with him and Ms. Piper. We agreed. The minute we sat down, Mr. Morani immediately accused me of lying. He said that I made it seem like it was Jean that put the water in my bag. I told him that I never said that it was her; I said that she touched my bag a few times in class. He went on to say that maybe I had a water bottle of my own in the book bag that had opened up and leaked. I started to get really upset and cry. I couldn't believe that now he was turning the tables on me and saying that I lied and wet my own things to make the bullies look bad! **What kind of a sick person was he? How dare he accuse me of making**

up a story to try to get the bullies in trouble when all of my things were destroyed in my wet bag! As if I would purposely pour a bottle of water in my bag to destroy my "BREAKING DAWN" BOOK just so I could make them look bad?

I didn't have enough hours in my day to figure out what is going to make these bullies look bad. As far as I was concerned, they were doing a good job of this themselves, and didn't need my help! My mom saw the ugly turn that this was taking, so she intervened and said Jamie never said that Jean poured water into her book bag! As a matter of fact she said that you wanted to know who touched her bag that day and she told you that it was Jean. My mom went on to say that it was her that said it looked like blue Gatorade, not me and that it was my dad who said it appeared to be water because it had no odor. You see there was no point at least a point that we could make! He was preparing to blame the whole incident on me and let Jean get away clean! Ms. Piper and Mr. Morani asked if I could please step out of the office so they could speak to my mom. Mr. Morani told my mom that he thought that I wasn't being totally truthful and that my story seemed to change a little. My mom told him that my story didn't change at all. As a matter of fact, my mom told him that he was too concerned with going back to his office that day because he had someone waiting for him in there, so he listened with one ear and then went back to his meeting and decided to write down what he thought he heard! My mom asked him if it was a sworn statement. He said no! My mom said "Good, because you wrote down what was convenient for you to write down, not what was the truth!" He didn't like that comment and with that he told my mom, that he, along with Ms. Piper, thought that I should be homeschooled. My mom told them that she had considered it, but once again she wanted the school to do something to punish the bullies instead of punishing me! Ms. Piper told my mom that she would set it up right away for me to be homeschooled, but my mom told them that she was going to talk it over with my dad and me and then make a final decision. Mr. Morani went on to say that he spoke with Jean's mother and she said that she was going to sue us for harassing her daughter! My mom said "Really?" So, is this what you're condoning Mr. Morani?". My mom told him "You

go right ahead Nr. Morani and tell her to sue me and my family and

I will make sure that your reputation is ruined for life!" My mom

said "So, is this how you planned on getting my daughter out of this

school and homeschooled?" He really had no comment except that

he had decided that he wasn't going to punish the kids who were

involved in the nasty I.M.s., because he and Ms. Piper weren't

positive that it came from Jeans computer even though it said her

web name on it! My mother had a few choice words for both of

them and it wasn't "Have a nice day!" As soon as we left the school,

I was hysterically crying. I couldn't believe what my mother told me

happened in that office. My mom said that Mr. Morani tried to make

it seem like I was accusing Jean and other kids of ruining my things

without seeing them do it. It was just another way for Mr. Morani to

be a MORON! I later found out that some of the kids who were

called down to the office for questioning said that they had seen a

few kids in the class with water bottles that day and they thought

that one of them was Jean! Amazing isn't it? I get accused of telling

In Jamie's Words

the principal and the assistant principal of all of the kids in that class that would have done something like this to me and then they go and turn the tables on me and say that I, in fact, accused them of destroying my personal property!

My mom was so scared of how I was behaving that she called the therapist's office to see if there was any way that she could see me right away. She told my mom that she could see me later that afternoon. My mom did some errands and then took me there. I was there for over an hour. I was extremely upset and distraught. I felt so incredibly betrayed and alone! I was hysterically crying, yelling and almost out of touch with reality. The therapist gave me a prescription for XANAX to try to calm me down. *As if this wasn't bad enough, while I was in the therapy session, my mom got a phone call from a tutor looking to set up times to come over to the house to start homeschooling me!* My mom couldn't believe it. She told the tutor that nothing was written in stone yet. She said that this was something that we were going to sit down and discuss again at a later date. You see, the school was really trying to push me out.

In Jamie's Words

I guess they figured it was easier to get rid of one kid rather than get rid of 22 kids that were bothering me on a daily basis! How sad, don't you think? I was literally at the mercy of the school! How could they want to get rid of a really good, smart, kind, conscientious kid and allow all the others to stay and continue bullying? This is why my parents went after the school district with their lawsuits. Even though the kids were bullying me all the time, the school was allowing it to take place. Even at times when they didn't need a witness to punish the kids, they would still go out of their way to call all the kids down to their office and question them. It was truly a way for them to try to discredit me, instead of finding the perpetrators! The next day I went to school and I wouldn't even look at Mr. Morani and Ms. Piper. Just the thought of being in the same building with them was turning my stomach! I would walk through the hallways in between classes and hear kids talking about me. I just kept walking and ignored it. I made a promise to myself to not allow these kids to bother me or torment me to that extent again. I kept telling myself that soon I would have my day, even if it is in a courtroom! I would win this battle not only for me and my family, but for all kids that have been bullied at one time or another!

At one point, someone had come up to me in class and told me that this girl Claire that I used to be friendly with, saw Mr. Morani and he told her that they wouldn't be seeing much of me anymore because I was leaving the school! I asked this girl if she knew who else was told this by Mr. Morani and she said Jean and Dylan. I wasn't so sure if I could trust what she said because I didn't really trust too many people at this point and I didn't know if she was just saying this to try to make me more upset! So I asked a few other kids if they had heard this story and they said yes! Can you imagine the assistant principal of the middle school going around school telling the bullies that they're not going to have to see me in the halls anymore? What kind of an IDIOT is he? Now he's spreading rumors about me too? This whole ordeal was really getting sick and twisted!! Besides whose side was he on? What gives Mr. Morani the right to release private information about me to the public whether it be true or false?

In Jamie's Words

I tried to get past all of these comments and rumors because it wasn't worth my time or energy. Once again, I kept telling myself that I was better than all of this, and truthfully I was!! A few days later, I was in gym and the teacher called me over and said "Now I know why you wanted your gym locker changed.". She said that she heard some things in the locker room that she didn't want to tell me. Okay, so why bring it up? She then said that she would keep an eye out for me. *So, let's get this straight! You call me over to talk to me, and you won't tell me what was said, but you're going to keep an eye out for me anyway? Listen, I know it's not me, but this is getting weirder every day!* The next night my mom and I went to the police to discuss the Aggravated Harassment charges against Jean and Dylan. We wanted to see if there was anything that the Crimes Unit could do for us. The detective was very nice, but wasn't willing to make the arrest because the girls were minors! Aren't you sick of this MINOR THING? I know that I was! What I didn't understand was that the DA's office and the County Attorney's office prosecute juvenile's every day, so why can't these cops arrest these girls for harassment? Are they just too lazy? Do they not want to do the paperwork? Once again, here I was lost in the shuffle! The only thing that the detective was willing to do was go to the girls' houses and speak with them and their parents. I was at least thankful for that! He told them that they had to leave me alone and if they didn't, then they would be arrested.

Needless to say, the next day it went around school that I called the cops on Jean and Dylan. I don't know about you, but if the cops came to my house to give my family and me a warning, you better believe that I wouldn't talk about it in school the next day! I just dealt with the gossip about the police and told kids that if they didn't leave me alone that I would do the same thing to them! My mom, on the other hand, did something really great! She made copies of all of the school education laws that were broken by the school principal, as well as the district and went up to school and personally handed them to Ms. Piper. She told her that these were the State Educational Laws and maybe she and Mr. Morani should brush up on them because they obviously didn't know them too well! Ms. Piper told my mother that she knew the laws well, but didn't think that the I.M.'s came from Jean's computer. My mom said "Really, who did they come from, Jean's mother?" My mom told her that the police knew who wrote them and that's why they went to their houses! Once again, this was another example of the unprofessionalism and incompetence of the principal! My family and I were really starting to feel targeted! It was the topic of everyone's conversation. What else could they do to us now? It was also becoming extremely obvious that the principal and assistant principal didn't want to help at all. It only got worse from here! The principal decided that she was going to SUSPEND ME!

My mom got a message on the answering machine from the superintendent. He said that he investigated some of the claims that I had made against Jean, Mary Jo and Clark and he decided to conclude that the incidents didn't have any merit, meaning "THEY NEVER HAPPENED!" What about all of the other zillion complaints that he never cared about? How about the most recent ones with the I.M.s from Jean, Dylan and Clark? I guess he was very selective when he chose the incidents to review! **The truth was that the district had just been served with the notice of claim to another lawsuit so he decided to retaliate against me and suspend me!** Mr. Butterman's decision to suspend me was only going to get him another notice of claim filed! It is against the law to retaliate against someone because of a lawsuit that was filed. My mom called Mr. Butterman's office to schedule a hearing because of the suspension, while my dad went to school to meet with the principal regarding this matter.

When I was leaving school that day, Ms. Piper came over to me and said "Remember Jamie, you have suspension tomorrow!" I said to her, "I HOPE YOU HAVE A GOOD ATTORNEY BECAUSE YOU'RE GOING TO NEED ONE!" She didn't like that comment very much, in fact she said "For that comment you deserve another day of suspension!" I laughed at her and walked out of the school onto the bus. At that very moment I felt really proud of myself for answering her back and not letting her get the best of me! I knew that my parents weren't going to be angry at me for

In Jamie's Words

answering her back. She so deserved it! The next morning my dad took me to school and we met my advocate there. We went over some things and then proceeded into the school's office. Mr. Morani didn't know who my advocate was, so he was reluctant to talk to him. They had some choice words back and forth between the three of them, but the end result was that we never had a conference regarding my suspension, nor were we able to question any of the parties involved until after the fact. This makes the suspension illegal. I had been sent to the suspension room while my dad, the advocate and Mr. Morani battled it out. At that point I was very upset that they were still suspending me without a hearing beforehand. I sat in the suspension room with a whole bunch of kids that were bullying and assaulting other kids on a daily basis. Then there was me, an innocent victim of bullying and abuse and they decided to punish me! They wouldn't let me call my therapist or my attorney. As a matter of fact, some of my teachers came to the suspension room to visit me and couldn't believe that I was really there. They kept saying that it must have been a mistake! I was such

In Jamie's Words

a good kid, why was I being punished? **RETALIATION was the reason for the punishment and hopefully all the people involved in this underhanded scheme would get theirs!** In the mean time, my dad and my advocate were still battling it out in the office while my mom was waiting at home for the district to call back with the information about the hearing that we were supposed to have before the suspension took place. **This was another example of the way this district operated. I was truly being "Legally Kidnapped!"** My dad and the advocate left the middle school completely frustrated, while I sat in a room with a bunch of delinquents! All I kept telling myself while I was in that suspension room was that my family and I would prevail! Even if it took awhile, we would come out ahead! The day was finally over and I was on my way home. When I arrived, my mom told me what had transpired with my dad and my advocate at the school as well as telling me that she made an appointment for a hearing at the district office. With that being said, I heard a knock at the door; it was someone from the district office looking to hand my mom a letter telling her that I was going to be suspended. My mom laughed at the man and told him that the suspension had already been served and he was a little late! She took the letter from him and asked him to sign the envelope with the date and time he arrived at our home. This way when we went to court it would be added into evidence to show that the letter came after the fact, not before. What I don't understand, is WHY? Why would a school go through so much trouble to retaliate against me when all they had to do was make things right? Don't they have a conscience? Don't they care about what's right or wrong? Didn't they realize that what they had allowed to happen to me would change my life forever? Weren't they the least bit concerned about what kind of impact this suspension was going to have on me, or were they trying to get even because we sued them for not protecting me in the first place?

SOMETIMES IT MAKES ME WONDER WHAT KIND OF PEOPLE THE WORLD IS REALLY MADE UP OF! A few days later we were scheduled to have this meeting to discuss the suspension. My mom made all of the necessary phone calls to our

In Jamie's Words

attorney's office as well as to George the advocate. She made sure that they would be present for this meeting. On the day of the meeting, I went to school, but my parents signed me out early so that I could be there. When we arrived at the district office we met with our attorney and my advocate. We went over some things briefly and then we went inside. As soon as we arrived, the front desk called back to Mr. Butterman to tell him that we were there and that we brought other people with us. Mr. Butterman came rushing to the front desk with a look of panic on his face. He said to my mom that our attorney wouldn't be allowed in because his attorney wasn't present. So, he allowed my mom, dad and my advocate in. They asked the rest of us which included myself, my grandmother and my attorney to please wait in the waiting area by the front desk. That was okay with me even though I was ready to give them a mouthful I think that my mom was ready to read them the riot act and put them in their place. Even though we weren't present in the meeting, after the fact we knew exactly what was said and where we were going with it all because my dad had tape-recorded the whole

In Jamie's Words

conversation loud and clear! It's amazing; because the whole beginning of the meeting Mr. Butterman repeatedly asks the advocate to put his phone away for fear that he was recording the conversation and sending it to the attorney in the waiting room! He cared more about the tape recording than he did about human life! It just goes to show what kind of people we're dealing with.

Little did they know that my dad had his Blackberry turned upside down the whole time so that he could record everything, without anyone realizing it. The next part of the conversation went like this… My mom asked Mr. Morani why he never spoke with Ms. Rosario regarding any of the incidents with Clark. My mom was very annoyed that while all of this bullying was going on, the assistant principal kept calling down the bully who kept denying it. My parents were fuming at the fact that Mr. Morani trusted what the bully said, which of course was that he didn't bother me! My mom kept saying "HOW COULD YOU TRUST A BULLY OVER MY DAUGHTER OR THE TESTIMONY OF A TEACHER?" Mr.

In Jamie's Words

Morani repeatedly said that I was a liar and the bully was telling the truth!

What kind of sick, twisted people are we dealing with? This was a total disgrace! Soon, it turned into somewhat of a screaming match. My parents wanted to get the suspension thrown out due to the fact that it had no merit. The three stooges saw it differently! They kept saying that I was a liar and the incidents that I reported were not true and that is why I was suspended. So let's get this straight; you suspend me because you couldn't do your homework properly to find the culprits that poured the water into my book bag and you kept questioning the wrong Clark... and I'm punished? Maybe you should be punished for being a complete imbecile!! The next part of the conversation wasn't any better. Ms. Piper said that she should have given me another day of suspension due to the fact that I told her that I hoped she had a good attorney. My mom said "What did you expect Jamie to say to you when you told her that she was being suspended because she lied about being bullied?"

In Jamie's Words

The next part was pretty intense. My mom was telling Mr. Morani that he didn't know how to do his job and that she felt that he was completely incompetent! My mom wanted to know why he didn't watch the videos in the hallways. You see, if he did he would have seen who it was stealing all of my things out of my locker and who it was that poured the water into my book bag. They probably would've been laughing behind me as all of the water was pouring out as I walked to my next class! Mr. Morani's answer was that the cameras were broken. My mom said "Really? That's interesting Mr. Morani because the first time we asked you to view the video cameras you said that you didn't have enough time and that it would take you all day. The second time we told you that we would come in and view the cameras ourselves, until we identified the kids, you said that it would be a violation of their rights if we looked at the cameras. The third time we asked you to view the cameras you told us that you rewound them. Now you're telling us that the cameras are broken? Who's lying now Mr. Morani? My mom was trying to demean him like he tried to do to me that day in his office when he was accusing me of lying about Jean pouring water into my book bag. My mother was trying to insinuate that it is a violation of every child's protection not to have cameras that work. Mr. Morani really had no comment after that regarding the video cameras. But then my dad got rolling and started to tell Mr. Morani that he doesn't know how to do his job and given the opportunity my dad could better. So that went back and forth for a few minutes until Mr. Butterman said we weren't getting anywhere. That is until my mom went nuts on Mr. Morani for allowing all of the Instant Messages and e-mails to go without punishment including the one about me wearing the "D**K HAT" while other kids dance around me singing the FUN song! My mom was non-stop, giving it to him, while the other two idiots were sitting there looking at my mom in shock. Honestly, I think that if I would have been in the room at that very moment that I would have given my mother a standing ovation for her performance! She repeatedly attacked him and said "MAYBE YOU SHOULD WEAR THE D**K HAT AND WE SHOULD PAY PEOPLE TO DANCE AROUND YOU AND SING THE FUN

In Jamie's Words

SONG!" My mom said, "Would you like that Mr. Morani? Don't you dare tell me that saying those things are not threatening or hurtful and don't deserve a severe punishment?" Obviously, my mom made her point because Mr. Morani finally said loud and clear "OKAY, YOU MADE YOUR POINT!" And so we did! We'll take that statement all the way to the bank, because that's exactly where will be headed when these lawsuits are finished! As my parents left the meeting room you could hear a pin drop. The air was thick with tension, but yet no words were spoken until my mom and dad headed for the door. They opened the door and started to close it behind them when they heard Mr. Butterman tell my advocate that he should be careful who he represents because we sue everyone! My mom and dad continued out the door and headed to the front desk were everyone was waiting for the outcome. We gathered outside in the parking lot and all took a listen to the damning evidence that we had from this Godforsaken meeting!

In our minds we were still ready for another fight, but in our hearts we knew that their day would come where they would have to defend themselves to a courtroom filled with people for their actions. Remember, they can say whatever they want, but we had the truth on tape and we would let the truth be told, and let justice be served!

In Jamie's Words

CHAPTER NINE

40 ANTI-BULLY TACTICS THAT SAVED MY

LIFE!

"KIDS' TACTICS"

1. Kids, tell your parents what's going on. If you don't want to tell your parents, don't be afraid to tell another adult that you're being bullied.

2. Tell your teacher, the bus driver, your guidance counselor. Don't be worried about telling on the kids. Don't be afraid to call the bus company if the incident happened on the bus. All buses are equipped with cameras so if something takes place on the bus, they will be able to rewind the tape and watch it.

3. If you don't get the response you're looking for from the teachers or guidance counselors – go to the principal, or assistant principal.

4. If the principal doesn't want to get involved, have your parents go to the District Office to speak with the superintendent. When you arrive, fill out a Harassment Incident Form, so that it's documented, and make sure you have someone make a copy for you so that you can keep it for your records.

5. If you're being threatened over the internet, learn how to save instant messages on your computer and cell phone, and emails on your computer and cell phone. Some messages that come across the

internet from the bullies can be used as evidence. Go to the police department and show the officer your printed messages for possible harassment charges. If you don't know how to save IM's, call AOL Fraud Dept. for instructions. If you are being harassed over Facebook, you must contact Facebook and let them know. Print these messages out as well and contact the police department's "Hate Crimes Unit" or ask the officer to connect you to the "Internet Crimes Division."

6. If nasty IMs or emails persist, save them and print them out. Show them to the principal at your school as evidence. Go to your local police department with them and have them write up a police report with a claim number. If the police officer doesn't want to get involved because the kids are minors, ask the officer to write up an "APPEARANCE TICKET." An appearance ticket will get these troublemakers into Family Court for an appearance. It's like making an arrest on a juvenile. Depending on the outcome, these kids could

get "PROBATION" for the acts that they have committed against you even if they are under the age of 16.

7. If the bullying continues and the school District isn't willing to help you, DON'T GIVE UP!

8. Be careful which friends you discuss your bullying situation with, because you don't know who you can trust. Even your closest friend(s) can turn on you. Some parents, as ridiculous as it may sound, actually tell their kids to befriend the bully so that they don't get bullied. I'm not telling you to do that, I think that befriending the bully so you don't get bullied is a bad idea.

9. Try to keep a positive outlook on life as well as in school, even though it's hard to stay focused. You may start to fail tests, so try to concentrate on your work. You need to take a good look around at all the kids in your grade and try to make new friends.

10. Find a hobby that you enjoy and go with it. Join a new club at school. Take an extra dance class, join a local theater and be in a play. Get involved in a sport after school. Take karate. Keep your mind occupied so you don't fall into depression. The sky is the limit!

11. Plan a really great vacation for you and your family! This will help get you mind off of the bullies and onto having some fun!

12. If you become depressed, definitely seek counseling. You can benefit from talking to a complete stranger who is unbiased about the situation. They can teach you good coping skills. Counseling is essential in your healing process.

13. Take pictures of any marks or bruises on your body that were a direct result of the bullying or physical abuse.

14. If you're having problems with the kids at the lunch table, speak to your principal about "table jumping" to other tables so that you can make new friends until you find a table that you're happy with.

15. If you can't table jump, then ask the principal about changing your lunch period, or ask the principal or guidance counselor if you could have your lunch in the library instead. If this still doesn't work, bring a good book with you to read during lunch.

16. Consider journaling! It's a good way to vent. Write about things that the troublemakers are doing and what you did about it. Also, include new friends you've made and the fun things you did in class and outside of class.

17. Carry a tape recorder, or cell phone that records and record all conversations in school that pertain to all the rumors and hearsay that apply to you.

18. Your other option is to have your parents remove you from the school and place you in a private school. This will be a costly choice. If you decide to do this, take the time to search for scholarships on your computer using **google.com**. This way you can try to get a few different scholarships to help pay for the private school, while you sue the school district for **endangering the welfare of a child and not providing the proper education that you as a child deserves, and Defamation of Character if it applies.** Your other option is to be homeschooled. If you're in therapy for the bullying, ask the therapist or psychiatrist to write a letter to the school requesting that you be homeschooled. Then, your advocate or attorney can set up a CSE Hearing (Committee for Special Education) at the district to have you relocated to a new school or be homeschooled, or you can discuss other options with your advocate with regard to switching schools and getting tuition reimbursement.

In Jamie's Words

19. Spend quality time with one of your parents for approximately 30-40 minutes a day. This quality time will pay off. Try to do something special together. Go to the park, take a walk together, go on a bike ride, go fishing, sit and polish each other's nails or go outside and throw a football around. Whatever it may be, try to make that special time for your child because it will let him or her know that you care and that you are there for them. Parents, try to give your child this time together. It is beneficial in his/her healing process and it will give you both a wonderful bond!

20. Make a list of all of your good qualities. Take a look at them every day. Learn to believe in yourself and feel good about who you are!

21. Leave all windows of opportunity open. Don't shut doors on people unless you have no interest in rectifying your situation with them.

22. Introduce yourself to new people. Even though you might be nervous, at first, say hello and try to make a new friend.

23. Try to think outside the box. Take yourself out of the situation, mentally, and imagine you're in a better place.

24. Don't let anyone intimidate you. Stand up to them and say what's on your mind without getting too carried away. Chances are, they will back off and walk away.

In Jamie's Words

"PARENTS TACTICS"

1. Parents, talk to your kids about being bullied, because if you think it won't happen to them...*you're wrong.*

2. Make a time line – write all incidents down – date, time, place, who you spoke to. This will come in handy when you go to the superintendent's office for a meeting or you need to contact the police and you need an accurate list of the events that took place.

3. If an email, IM, or Facebook message is sent to you or your child with threats or harassing material, you must save it and contact the police and see what they can do about arresting that individual due to Cyber-Bullying laws in that county. If you don't save it, you can discuss the option with the police department to get a subpoena to retrieve the email as evidence.

In Jamie's Words

4. If you live in New York, contact the Center for School safety in Albany at 845-255-8989 or nyscenterforschoolsafety.org and report the incidents in hopes that they will investigate the school and the principal. They can advise you of what the rules are within the district. If you don't live in New York, you should contact them for a phone number for a center within your state.

5. Hire an advocate. He or she can represent you in the school district to try to get needs met, or call a hearing to rearrange your child's schedule or bus route for a safer, more educational day at school. This is an important step in your child's recovery.

6. If you have or your child has been discriminated against for race, color, religion, gender, etc. contact the US Department of Education Office of Civil Rights. Print out the blank incident report, fill it in and send it back to them so that they may start their investigation. You may also contact your state's Human Rights Bureau and fill out a complaint as well for them to investigate the incident.

7. Consult with an attorney that specializes in Educational Law. This way you will know what rights and laws have been violated. Our attorney's name is Mitchell Carlinsky, he can be reached at: 516-622-0099. You can also reach him by mail at Carlinsky, Dunn and Pasquarillo, PLLC, 8 Duffy Avenue, Hicksville New York 11801.

8. Go to the district office and request a copy of your child's records, grades, transcripts, etc. This will enable you to have all of the documents that are in your child's folder on file. By law once you have filled out a FOIL form, the district must provide the documents that you requested even if you have to wait up to 2 weeks for them to arrive.

9. If you are looking for a therapist and don't know where to go, you should first research in your neighborhood for a teen youth center for counseling. If you are unsuccessful, call your health insurance provider for participating therapists.

In Jamie's Words

10. Request a school bus monitor or attendant to be on the bus if the bullying continues.

11. Go to your public library and take a look at "Educational Law" books. These books are found in the reference section of the library and are not permitted to leave so be prepared with change to make copies of all laws that pertain to you. This will give you knowledge of all of the state educational laws and how they affect your situation.

12. Write a letter to the Commissioner of the US Department of Education in your state. See if there is anything that he or she can do to help you resolve your child's situation.

13. If you live in New York State you can go online to www.highered.nysed.gov and fill out a Moral Character Complaint Form against the teacher, principal or even the superintendent. If

you are not in New York, please access your State Department of Education website.

14. Do some research to find out who is the president of your county's Council of School Superintendents. Contact that person so you can gather information to make a complaint about your schools superintendent.

15. If you're at the point that we were at and you don't care about exposing your situation to the TV networks and the news, get in touch with your local newspaper and news channel to tell your story. Sometimes it won't only benefit you, but anyone else in your shoes that have been afraid to come forward with a similar situation.

16. Reach out to political figures like Legislators and Senators, or your local town Mayor. Tell them your story. See how they respond to you and your letters or emails, then schedule an appointment to

In Jamie's Words

meet with them so that they might write a letter to the school on

your behalf, but whatever you choose to do DON'T GIVE UP!

In Jamie's Words

CHAPTER TEN

MY THEORY

JEALOUSY!!! That's my theory. Since I was a little girl I've always had people make comments about how I was dressed or how my underwear matched my outfit. In second grade it got worse. These girls who started bothering me used to be my friends. They would come over all the time. All the kids always wanted to have a play date at my house because they said that I had everything. I think that's the real reason for all of the animosity that started at a young age. Even when my mom tried to speak with some of the parents of the kids involved in the bullying, they all indicated to my mom that we were really rich. It's amazing! How would they know how much money we have or didn't have? Just because we have a beautiful home and I have nice clothes doesn't mean that we have a money tree growing in the back yard.

What I don't understand is how could their parents just sit back and let it happen? My mom and dad would be furious with me if I bullied someone. They would bring me to their house so I could apologize to the kid as well as the parents. How humiliating it would be! I would feel terrible if I hurt someone as bad as they hurt me. Instead, these girls got off on it.

Even today the bullying still goes on and more and more kids join in. I don't know why. Honestly, I would rather be alone with no friends than join in on the hazing and harassment of an innocent kid. It's hard for me sometimes to see their parents in a store because I truly don't know how they live in their own skin. How could they be proud of their child's accomplishments when their

261

In Jamie's Words

child went out of her way to try to hurt and humiliate another? It makes you wonder what kind of upbringing these girls had. Were they raised like animals? Did they have to fight or hunt for their food and shelter? It sure looks that way.

Don't they have a CONSCIENCE? Aren't they the least bit sorry? Is saying I'm sorry so difficult? If that's the case then the word SORRY must be the hardest word to spell in the dictionary! I actually find it disgusting that these girls can't just come up to me and say "JAMIE, I'M SORRY!" You would think saying that to me would almost be like cleansing their souls! Like beginning a new day! The word SORRY is a very powerful word. It can bring a person to tears just hearing someone say it. I guess that knowing that someone is sorry makes you feel like you've won the battle. Maybe?

One girl said that she was sorry in 7th grade. Did she mean it? Probably not! Alexandra would repeatedly try to befriend me after she hurt me, and if I didn't respond quickly with embracing her again then she would say something sarcastic to hurt me again. It was a vicious cycle. Nasty, Nice, Nasty, Nice! Give me a break!

In Jamie's Words

Pick one and stick with it. Obviously she is still searching for her identity, so therefore I've been her punching bag through her search. Honestly, I'm not going to be anyone's punching bag anymore. Like I said before, "I'd rather be alone than have a friend who was two-faced, or made me be a part of the two-faced click!

Can you imagine going through life picking on people? Checking out what they are wearing or what they look like? Maybe you don't like their hair or their make-up, or maybe they are too short or too tall. Maybe they're just not perfect like you! Isn't that what they are really saying? Or is it a cry for help? Personally, I never made fun of anyone. I could care less what they looked like or what kind of clothes they wore or if they were rich or poor. It didn't matter to me. I'm not a jealous person so therefore I don't judge people. I take them for what they are worth and I try to find their inner beauty and their inner strengths and that's what draws me to be their friend. It doesn't matter what a person looks like on the outside. It's what's on the inside that counts. Didn't their mothers or

In Jamie's Words

fathers ever teach them that? Maybe in the wild they didn't learn their manners.

I think that all these rotten kids just got off on harassing me. I honestly think that the kids that knew me well and have been to my home are truly jealous of me and my family life. What can I say? I am blessed with awesome parents and a really great brother and sister. I think that it might be too much for some kids to handle. Some of these kids come from really bad home situations. I guess it didn't matter how nice my mom or dad were to them because the results were all the same. As far as all of the other jerks that decided to chime in with these kids, they truly knew nothing about me, they just wanted to be part of the click. Once again, I pity them. They will never find true happiness in life if they are constantly comparing themselves to me. They have shallow minds and will grow up to continue to have shallow minds as long as they think and act the way they do.

Try to picture yourself in my shoes if you can. How would you feel? Would you be sad and depressed all the time? Would you

In Jamie's Words

spend most of your time thinking about ending your life? Maybe you wouldn't want to come out of your room or leave your house to go to school? I would have to say that all of these would probably be the normal reactions to this situation, but then who wins? You or them? So, please, if you're having any of these depressed feelings because of your bullying issues, try to find your inner strength to pull you through. Look beyond the sadness and search for the beauty in you! Don't let anyone take away who you are and what you believe in because that's what they set out to do. Don't give them what they want. Instead show them that you're not going to cave in because of their selfish and dysfunctional acts. Show them that you will rise above all of this garbage because that's all it is and ever was! Make them feel like garbage because that's what they truly are!

So, does it really matter what my theory is? Probably not! Do all of the immature kids that hurt me really matter? Absolutely not! Do the teachers and the principal that allowed all of this to happen matter? YES! Absolutely yes! Shame on them if they didn't care enough to go that extra mile to give me the education that I deserved

In Jamie's Words

in a safe environment. Shame on them for not taking a stand and making a change in the school or in the classroom for me. Shame on them for not protecting me from the enemy or enemies while on school property. Someone has to bear the responsibility for these actions and for this reason you must hire the best educational attorney that you can find to represent you and your family.

Just remember the road may be long, but in the end you will prevail. Please don't give up! Some days the sun shines down on us and some days the clouds roll in. We must not give up the fight for what we believe is right and just. Keep your head held high and be proud of who you are and don't let anyone ever change that. One day it will all be behind you and you will have risen above it all, and so will I! As far as these kids, their memories of their education will be filled with emptiness and regret for not saying they were sorry for what they had done.

CHAPTER ELEVEN

MY MOM'S THEORY

My mom's theory is pretty simple. You see, I'm not ugly, fat, or have any kind of **outstanding** features that would make someone want to make fun of me. I just have a lot going for me and I guess that it made me the perfect target. My mom says that not only me, but also my brother and sister are all a "**COMPLETE PACKAGE!**" What she means by this is that we come from a loving and happy home. My parents don't fight and we all have a lot

In Jamie's Words

of respect for each other. We dress really nice, most of the time in fashionable clothing. We try to eat dinner together as much as possible and it's always something really good. My parents aren't drunks or drug addicts, nor do they allow us to roam the streets at night. You'll never see me hanging out on a street corner like you do the **BULLIES!**

So, basically, my mom thinks that this makes it even more the reason for me and my family to be targets for bullying! My mom and dad have spent a lot of time raising us the right way and giving us the attention that not only we deserve, but that we need to grow! **AS A FAMILY WE ARE EXTREMELY STABLE! AS AN INDIVIDUAL, I AM VERY CONFIDENT, STABLE and MATURE!** I owe this to the love and support that my parents have given me.

Even though the bulling went on for 5 years, I never took it personally! Don't get me wrong; it bothered me every day, every second of my life and especially my mom's life! What I mean is, I never looked in the mirror and said "You're ugly or fat, or worse than that...I don't want to live anymore!" These words never entered my mind, nor did they ever come out of my mouth! *I just felt an unbelievable amount of anxiety and depression.* There was a time when I didn't want to leave the house or do anything. I just wanted to stay in my bedroom and cry! The pain and hurt was so unbearable for me and my mom. My mom was right there for me the whole time. Most of the time she couldn't believe what was happening and why it wouldn't stop.

After **UNCOUNTABLE** visits with the principal and comments such as *"Why don't you pull Jamie out of this school and put her in private school", my mom realized that they all must have thought that we were really wealthy and if we wanted the bulling to stop, then we had to pay for it to stop!* How ridiculous is that? We had heard from other kids as well as their parents that the principal had comments about us behind our backs. You're not allowed to discuss other children and their circumstances with other families. Who gave her permission to DEFAME US? Didn't she realize that not only was she defaming us, but she was putting our lives at risk!

In Jamie's Words

What if we did this to her? What if we spread rumors about her to the whole school community, would she like that? DIDN'T SHE REALIZE THAT SHE WAS HOLDING THE KEY TO END THE BULLYING? All she had to do was do the right thing and use her key to get the bulling to stop! But, she didn't! Didn't she care enough about her own reputation or was she too busy trying to ruin mine?

My mom would never be able to live with herself if she allowed all of these bad things to repeatedly happen to an innocent child. Up to this day my mom doesn't know why none of these kids or their parents could bring themselves to ring our doorbell and say they were SORRY. How did they go through their daily routine and look themselves in the mirror and not feel SORROW or REMORSE? MY FAMILY AND I PITY THEM! How terrible it must be to carry around all that guilt. I would never be able to carry that with me for the rest of my life, but that's what makes us different. I actually have a conscience! Aside from that, my family

In Jamie's Words

and I have a lot of pride and that's what is giving us the tools to succeed!

Getting back to the "complete package theory," did I mention that we're big animal lovers and we had two horses? One of them lived with us for a little while. It was a very exciting time for us. Gibraltar lived with us in our yard in a barn that my dad and cousin built. In passing comments told to me when I was in 2nd grade, they always referenced the fact that we must be really rich to have horses. Yeah, we were so rich that we donated the horses a few years ago. It was a very upsetting time especially for my mom to give up the horses. It was becoming very difficult to care for them and take care of this bullying problem, which had become more than a full time job! My mom felt as though she was giving up her children. She made sure that we gave them to a place that would care for them the way we did and would love them as deeply and unconditionally as we did. We all knew in our hearts that we did the right thing for them. It wouldn't have been fair not to give them the time that they needed due to constant turmoil that was in our lives. It's just very sad that it had to come to that!

My mom and I aren't sure why people are always looking to judge you because they perceive you to be a certain way. It makes my mom nuts to constantly defend herself financially. What I mean is – when was the last time these people checked our bank account? Why were they so concerned with how much money we had? For God sakes, even the principal of the elementary school perceived us as being really wealthy! Our tax dollars pay her salary, so don't you think that when she kept making comments to us about moving me into a private school she should have been more humble? Maybe instead of thinking that we were really rich, she should've been kind and said, "Sure Mr. and Mrs. Isaacs, I will get to the bottom of this situation for you!" After all, it's her job, isn't it? Or is it her job to waste our tax dollars and in return give us nothing but grief?

This is why my mom was so angry! Not only was I being bullied severely and my brother was having all of his stuff stolen in school at the hands of the same principal, but all of our hard earned money was being wasted on an education I never got! How dare they use our tax dollars to pay the salaries of these teachers who were chiming in with the bullies and making fun of me? The district wasn't any better. They would just continue to tell us what we wanted to hear, but then when my parents walked out the door, nothing was done! **My mom felt as though by using our tax dollars to pay the salaries of the teachers and the principal we were almost paying for the bullying!** If you take a good look at my situation you will see that there is so much more to it than just bullying! There was much jealousy and hate among the kids who bothered me. There was loyalty between the teachers, the principal and the district to stick together and not help and do what was right for us, only what was right for them! There was also a lot of covering up going on. A lot of the parents whose kids were bullying me belonged to the PTA. My mom couldn't stand going to the PTA meetings with all of those two-faced people pretending to care about the kids and the school. All they cared about was their own popularity and the popularity of their child. It turned out that they

In Jamie's Words

were all in it for a hand out, even the principal. My mom and dad had spoken to a few parents who confirmed that the principal of the elementary school was taking funds for her own use from the PTA fundraisers while allowing the kids who were bothering me to continue on while she looked the other way, just like the parents involved with her skimming looked the other way!

So, what do you think so far? Do you think that my mom's theory is correct? Do you think that maybe we were getting in the way of the principal's plans? The next situation that really turned my parents' stomachs was that all of these kids and their families don't like Jews! My mom is Italian Catholic and my dad is a Polish Jew. My brother, my sister and I were baptized and had a baby naming. We are raised Catholic, but celebrate all of the Jewish holidays. This is something that we really enjoy. We look forward to each holiday because we know that it's more family time that we get to spend together! My brother and I have heard so many racial slurs because we're part Jewish. My mom feels as though these kids must think that after they've called us all the names they can think of,

In Jamie's Words

now it's time to insult our faith! As you've already read in chapter seven, even the elementary school principal found it necessary to insult our faith. Can you imagine that the principal would stoop that low, and commit a BIAS CRIME! Basically, it was like a free for all! If the principal could defame us, why not allow all the kids to chime in too? The big question is WHY IS SHE STILL A PRINCIPAL? Didn't she realize that my parents were going to pursue this to the fullest? Didn't the district realize that they were digging their own grave? I guess not, because the bullying was about to continue after my brother would enter 6th grade in that same God-forsaken school!

Get ready to see what my parents are all about and the path they chose to set me free and save us from these demons!

CHAPTER TWELVE

"THE NEW BEGINNING"

My mom and dad enrolled me in a private college prep school. I couldn't wait!! I was filled with so much excitement. I had embraced the fact that my life was about to change! I loved the fact that I was getting a private bus to take me back and forth to school that was bully free! I loved the fact that there would only be a few kids per class and that the personalized attention would be like having my own tutor!

In Jamie's Words

Every morning I enjoy looking out the window of the bus as I head for school. I feel like such a weight has been lifted off of my chest. I feel like I'm alive! I feel like my voice is heard! I have a new take on life and I'm happy to get up in the morning and start my day! I always saw the true beauty of life, but now I appreciate it, and I owe it all to my parents and to the Knox School for this incredible opportunity!

When approaching the Knox School, you feel like you have just entered into the most beautiful retreat. It was an old estate that has been converted into a coed college prep school. The horse stables are on the left with horses grazing in their paddock. On the right are larger paddocks with more horses and beautiful green pasture. As you pull further in, you see some of the dorms and smaller cottages, which the classrooms are in. Overall, the school's appearance is so peaceful.

I love everything about the school, even the dining experience. I feel like I'm a princess in an old Victorian mansion with high ceilings and long curtains on the windows. This is a big

In Jamie's Words

change from a cafeteria filled with bullies that would demean me the second I walked in, or throw food at me if they didn't like what I was wearing, or what I had to say!

I can't believe that I'm treated with respect by everyone. If I have a question or a problem, my voice is heard. I'm not a speck of dust that goes unnoticed! I looked forward to all of the opportunities that this school had to offer, as well as all of the lasting friendships, but something very ugly was about to change the meaning of peace and tranquility very soon.

While I was enjoying my new life and trying to overcome all of my demons, my brother, Danny, was about to experience what I had been through with these bullies first hand. My mom wanted to put him in private school for middle and high school while my dad didn't think that Danny would be bullied in middle school because of his size. Because my brother towers over people, including most of the teachers, my dad felt confident that Danny would be left alone. My mom on the other hand, felt the complete opposite and knew that once these kids saw that I wasn't coming back to school

In Jamie's Words

to continue on with them into 8th grade, they would then turn to Danny as their new victim.

On the first day of 6th grade, Danny walked to the corner and got onto the bus. He wasn't nervous at all, just excited about seeing some of his old friends that he had to leave behind when he got moved in 4th grade to the other elementary school. Danny proudly looked for a seat and sat down. About a minute later, Amelia stepped onto the bus with some friends. Suddenly, Amelia and her friends approached Danny and said "Hey Danny, where's your sister?" Do you remember when I used to come over all of the time and I took your Hermit Crab and purposely dropped him on the floor and his legs fell off? I killed him, didn't I? Well, I'm gonna get rid of you just like I got rid of your sister!" My brother could feel his heart beating out of his chest. He looked around to see if anyone had a comment about what Amelia and her "posse" had to say to him, but no one did. My brother had no come back. He figured if he said anything, it would only get worse so he tried to ignore them.

281

In Jamie's Words

The bus finally pulled into the school. It felt like it took an hour! My brother started to feel like he was trapped in a sardine can with piranhas! When the bus doors opened, he hopped off quickly and went to class. As the day went on he forgot about Amelia and caught up with some of his buddies that he hadn't seen in a while. Everyone was really happy to see him yelling "Hey Big D, is that you?" My bother enjoyed seeing everybody that he had to leave behind. Suddenly, the day was over and my brother realized that he was headed for the bus again. He got on and sat quietly. Amelia got on and started right in with her "BS." Once again, my brother kept quiet and refused to make eye contact with her. She was still so scrawny just like he had remembered but only older and more brazen. All he thought about was getting home and getting away from her! That whole day I had a knot in my stomach thinking about my brother and if he was ok. As soon as I got home, he told me about his day and what Amelia and her "posse" did. My mom had this sick look on her face. She knew that it was going to happen like this. It was more than mother's intuition; it was like she was

In Jamie's Words

psychic. She tried to make very light of it, hoping that my brother wouldn't dwell on it like I did and get swallowed up in it.

When my dad got home, my brother told him what happened with Amelia. My dad was actually surprised to hear that she started in with Danny because of his size and the fact that he's a boy. You would think she wouldn't waste her time bullying him because there were other girls she could have destroyed. My dad gave Danny some advice and told him to just ignore her because she was looking for a rise out of him. We sat down for dinner and discussed the situation in depth. You could see the tension in my mom's face, like she wanted to reach over the table and strangle my dad for keeping my brother in that school, but she was trying to compose herself.

As the days went on so did the abuse from Amelia. We were all getting really tired of it and the ignoring wasn't working. I rarely saw my parents argue. For the most part they always got along, even when things were pretty bad with me, but now I was seeing them have longer and louder discussions. My mom was really upset that my dad wasn't siding with her and my dad just wanted my mom to

In Jamie's Words

understand that he was proving a point. But proving it to whom? My dad wanted to see if the bullying was going to continue with Danny involving the same group of kids that bothered me. He had spoken to a few other attorneys that told him that this would be an ace in the hole if the same kids continued to bother the same family. *Well, the test results were in and they were accurate about these kids wanting to finish the job in getting at the Isaacs family.* I realized that my brother was going to suffer the wrath that I endured and now he was stuck in that school. My mom called every private school on Long Island and no one could take him because the private schools started in high school not middle school. Knox said that they would take him but they didn't have a football team, so the move wouldn't have been the right one because he wants to be a professional football player. We now felt really trapped... as if we haven't had this feeling before?

The only other option seemed to be homeschooling and we didn't want to do that. Some kids are good candidates for homeschooling, but my brother really needs to socialize and my parents didn't want to take that away from him as of yet. Now my mom was determined to get the school to move Danny to another one of their middle schools. So once again my mom started to make a timeline of events that took place on a daily basis with these bullies. At one point my brother got threatened on the bus by the "posse" without Amelia present, which now included several more boys than girls. I guess because of my brother's size they figured they better get more muscle. My brother still hadn't responded to anything they were doing.

The next day the same thing happened on the bus, and the next day, and the next day and the next. This went on for weeks. My mom and dad still hadn't called the school because they were hoping that eventually she would get sick of bothering him and he, having no response, would make her just give up. My mom didn't want to sound the alarms yet; she was going to wait for more to happen before she got out the big guns!

My brother was getting to the end of his rope. He couldn't take the abuse anymore. Amelia wasn't on the bus anymore because

In Jamie's Words

she was at cheerleading practice, but she made sure that this kid Newman followed her orders. Newman was crazy about her and would do anything for her if she would just give him the time of day. But he didn't realize that she's just a user and she only wanted to keep the momentum going. Finally, Danny got to the breaking point and started to record what Newman was provoking the kids in the back of the bus to say and do. Newman was getting them to yell inappropriate sexual comments to Danny and the whole back of the bus was chiming in. My brother taped it all and when he came home, he played it for us. Finally, what we've been waiting for…proof that there was bullying going on - on the bus.

The next morning my mom called the 6th grade guidance counselor Mrs. Thompson (the same woman who was my guidance counselor) and told her that she needed to come in to discuss a situation that happened on the bus and that my brother would be coming in with her. When they arrived my dad was with them and they went straight into guidance. After hearing the recording on Danny's phone the Mrs. Thompson asked if she could take the

286

In Jamie's Words

phone into Mr. Morani's office and play it for him. My mom and dad had no problem with that providing that he didn't tell Newman and his buddies where the recording came from. My mom and dad signed a harassment complaint form that the guidance counselor had given us. She assured us that the situation would be handled so there was no reason to take Danny back home with them. They left my brother at school to finish out his day. At the end of the day Danny got his phone back from Mr. Morani. He proceeded with caution as he climbed the bus stairs, only to be greeted by Newman and a few other boys who had been chiming in on the bus. Danny tried to walk past them but they stopped him and asked why he "ratted" them out to Mr. Morani. Danny was startled to see them; after all, the guidance counselor told Danny and my parents that there was no reason to be concerned, that she took care of it and the boys involved would be reprimanded. If the boys were going to be punished for what they did, why were they on the bus? Well, Newman and buddy Sean decided to demand sexual favors from Danny because he was Jewish. They told him that Jews perform sexual acts on other boys. Danny told them to back off, but they continued with their racist, sexual comments. My brother told the bus driver, but as usual he did nothing. As soon as Danny got off the bus he ran home. He flung open the door and threw his backpack down and told my mom that he had had enough. He was furious that the school would put him in such a terrible predicament like that. My brother couldn't understand why the school would lie when they told him and my parents that these boys would be punished for the original crime. Why would the school do this? My mom took my brother to the police department again and spoke to the Bias Crime Unit. The officer told my mom that he would get right on it and speak to the superintendent because he had a decent relationship with him. In the meantime, the next morning my dad drove Danny to school and my mom called guidance and asked why she would promise us one thing and do another. Mrs. Thompson seemed confused but quickly covered her tracks. She told my mom that she didn't realize that these boys were going to torment Danny like that because they weren't told who provided the tape recording. What exactly does that mean? My mom asked why these boys were allowed to ride the bus home; she replied that she was unable to contact their parents. My mom was outraged...she flipped out on Mrs. Thompson telling her that she needed to call her in the event that the parents were unable to be contacted so that we could make other arrangements to pick Danny up to spare him the next round of abuse! Then Mrs. Thompson told my mom that she was sorry that she didn't give her that option. These boys could have hurt my brother. Then, would she have been sorry that she forgot to make that call? I don't understand the incompetence of people who are supposed to be the opposite.

The next day, these boys weren't on the bus ride home. We had no idea if they were on the bus ride to school, because my dad drove my brother each morning. We weren't taking any more chances. Now, once again, my parents had to be inconvenienced due to the ongoing harassment of the students, as well as the incompetence of the administration. Wow, were the bullies and their parents ever inconvenienced or did the school just conform to their needs? The police weren't any better; they never called my parents back to talk to them about the incident. I know for a fact that they did pay a visit to the middle school and speak with the principal and assistant principal but after that I have no idea what transpired.

After about two weeks, my brother saw the boys back on the bus ride home. Danny actually had some peace and quiet on the bus for a while; however, it didn't take too long before this group would reach out to other kids to bother my brother. By this time, Danny wasn't feeling very good. His asthma was really bad; he needed his inhaler all the time and his stomach was always upset. It was very difficult for me to watch and absorb. I felt so guilty I didn't know what to do. I almost didn't want to go to school and enjoy my day because I knew my brother was living in hell! I couldn't understand why these kids were abusing my brother like this. They wanted me not him so why were they continuing the abuse?

I also felt really bad for my mother; she was always upset even though she was trying to pretend that she was going to make it through ok. She tried really hard to be strong for my brother and kept telling him that it was going to get better, but I saw and understood what was happening underneath it all. My mom was so angry at my dad for allowing all of this to happen. I mean my dad didn't make my brother get bullied but he could have prevented it. I love my parents so much and I couldn't bear to see them so upset and angry with each other. I prayed every night that God would make things better and that he would get the bullying to stop so that I could have my family back.

The months were passing by now and my brother's health was getting worse and so was his weight and demeanor. My brother started to gain weight due to stress and this wasn't helping his asthma at all. Comments were still being said on the bus and now my brother was being harassed in the hallways by a group of 7th and 8th graders. He went to the office as well as guidance so many times to report the incidents, but as usual, nothing was done to control it. We were actually all surprised that Newman and Sean had been removed off the bus for 2 weeks because it was so unlike the school to do anything for us. I know that the only reason the principal and

In Jamie's Words

assistant principal did anything about the bus incident was because we had it on tape. What are we supposed to do …carry a tape recorder around with us all the time? I don't know how my brother focused at all. I couldn't even focus at my new school because he was always on my mind.

By this time, my mom was so disappointed in the school system and also in my dad. I think my dad was really feeling it too… you could see it in his face. My dad apologized to my mom several times for not listening to her, for wanting to put Danny in private school, but it wasn't doing us any good now. My mom had enough and the situation wasn't looking good. My mom was on a mission to clean up this mess once and for all; not only the mess at home but the huge mess at school. My dad was also very distraught. He kept telling my mom that he had to stop the insanity right away before it got the best of us.

CHAPTER THIRTEEN

THE FINAL STRAW

Danny's demeanor was quickly changing. He was so angry one minute and then so upset the next. He would blow up at us for no reason and then want to spend every second with my mom or dad. We even went through a period where he was blaming my mom for everything, almost to say that she cared more about me than him. My mom would cry all the time and tell him how much she loved him and how she would go to the end of the earth for him, but it wasn't enough. I think this is what was making it really bad for my mom because my dad was the one who had put his foot down and wanted him to stay in that middle school and my mom was the one that just wanted to start over, even if it meant that we had to re-finance the house again to pay for his private school education. My mom couldn't understand how Danny could be so angry at her.

Needless to say things weren't getting any better at school for him. Now one of his new friends that he had just met this year was starting to turn on him. We all saw it right away; Jose would come over and hang out with my brother, ride bikes, skateboards etc. until he started to ask a lot of questions about the kids who bothered me. He always wanted to stay for dinner so that he could look at my yearbook and try to make me rehash what happened. My mom started to ask him a lot of questions as well, such as "Why do you want to know so much information about what happened to Jamie?" He said because he felt bad about what happened to me. I wasn't buying it and neither was my mom. She knew that there was something up his sleeve. After he would leave, my mom would tell

In Jamie's Words

Danny to be extremely careful with Jose and don't trust him because he was up to something no good. My brother would listen but also take it with a grain of salt. Sadly, my brother would find out all too soon what Jose's true colors were.

It was November 2010 and Jose started being really rude to Danny on the bus for no reason. He started to get other kids against my brother. He would sit with this girl named Bambi who was a total slut. He would turn around and look at my brother on the bus and make these disgusting sexual faces and expressions. My brother couldn't believe that he was doing this. Then my brother found out, when he was cornered in the hall by a group of 7th and 8th graders, that Jose planned all of the incidents! Wow, did this shock all of us. My mom was proceeding with caution with Jose, but we had no idea that he had already plotted against Danny from the get go. My brother went to the office and told the principal what was going on and of course she called these kids down. They claimed that they were cornering Danny because he liked Bambi and they were protecting her. What! My brother, like Bambi? My brother freaked

296

In Jamie's Words

out in the office and said *"What are you talking about; I have no interest in Bambi."* Ms. Piper made my brother and the boys shake hands and go back to class. I don't approve of what she did at all. You're never supposed to put the victim in the same room with the bully because the bully always blames the victim. That's how they continue bullying. I also don't approve of what she did because they made my brother look like a fool by telling people that he liked a whore like Bambi. God forbid!

Now we were starting to see where this was all going. It started to look like Jose was approaching kids who bothered me so that he could turn them against my brother. He would sit on the bus while making those disgusting faces and when he got off the bus, he would whisper to my brother that he was going to "F***" Amelia so that she would do whatever he wanted so she would continue to harass Danny. Everyone knew that Amelia was a slut and that she would perform sexual favors to get what she wanted. This was getting a little ridiculous don't you think? How old are these kids...12? It goes back to the way these kids are raised. My parents didn't raise us like animals; we were raised with a lot of love and respect. We respect our bodies and don't use them as a tool to get what we want, especially at 12 or 13 years old!

My mom had contacted Ms. Piper to discuss what was going on, on the bus, with Jose. At first, she seemed concerned but that quickly changed. My mom also notified the bus company. She had now developed a really good relationship with the people there. The manager couldn't believe what was happening and couldn't understand why the school wasn't taking the right approach to diffuse this. If nothing else, he became a listening ear for my mom and was also able to rewind the videos on the bus to see exactly what was going on. But for whatever reason none of this mattered to the principal or the assistant principal. They really didn't care what was happening on the bus, nor did they care what was happening in school.

By now my brother was really uptight. He found himself eating like crazy, I guess to fill the void? Whatever the reason was, it wasn't good. My mom tried to talk to him and help him to realize that his now ferocious appetite was due to extreme anxiety. It didn't help; my brother was spiraling downward too fast to control. This was so difficult for me to witness. My heart was breaking and I couldn't control it. I had to go to school every day and get on with my life. I would try to leave my torment behind me and heal, while I was literally dying inside with the pain that my brother was going through. I would come home every day and talk to my brother for hours making sure that he was in a safe place mentally but he was still so sad about what was happening that he couldn't see the light. Honestly at that time I couldn't see the light for him either but we weren't giving up!

Kids were now coming up to my brother in the halls and telling him that Jose was talking trash about him. Kids were still following him through the halls saying mean things under their breath behind him as well as trashing him in the lunchroom. Why couldn't they just leave him alone? There was no escaping it, everywhere Danny went something was being said. My parents wrote letters to the superintendent about the behavior in the school and how it was continuing. We never received a response. My parents went to the middle school and spoke to Ms. Piper and Mr. Morani and still they refused to fix it. They told my parents that Jose didn't want to have anything to do with Danny and that Danny was so big, why was he afraid of Jose? My parents told them that that wasn't the point. It didn't matter how big Danny was, it was still affecting him academically and socially. My parents told them that Danny couldn't focus and couldn't pass tests because he was constantly being abused. This conversation was recorded and it's pretty sad to hear the assistant principal tell us that Danny was a big boy and that Jose was afraid of him. Talk about judging a book by its cover. It was so sad that this had to happen again, but it was about to get even worse.

It was December 23rd, and it was the last day of school before Christmas break. The sexual comments on the bus by Jose and Bambi were continuing and too much to handle. The mouth and hand gestures that Jose was making to Danny were so rude and vulgar. Danny would try to sit as far away as possible from them, but they would get up and move near Danny again. They would sit

in front of him and turn around and stare. At one point, Jose turned

to Danny and said that he was going to rape my mother and after he

was done he was going to come after me! My brother was busting.

He told Jose that he had better shut up and turn back around or else!

Jose just continued. My brother texted my dad and told him that he

wouldn't be getting off of the bus at our stop; he was getting off at

Jose's stop. He told my dad what Jose was saying and that he wasn't

going to take it anymore. My dad tried to tell Danny that he was

egging him on and to just get off at our stop, but Danny refused. He

just kept saying that he wasn't going to let Bambi and Jose continue

to harass him like this anymore! The bus stopped, and Jose got up

and Danny followed. They exited the bus and Jose turned around

and started mouthing off to Danny telling him that he had better stay

the hell away from him. My brother told him that he had better stay

far away from him and his family otherwise things were going to

change. Bambi just ran home and wanted no part of what was about

to take place. With that, Jose got in Danny's face and put his pointer finger on my brother's chest. That's all it took for Danny to unleash on him. My brother looked around to make sure that the bus had left and was nowhere in sight. With the coast clear, my brother grabbed Jose and put his arm around Jose's neck and lifted him off the ground. It happened so quickly that Jose didn't even know what hit him. My brother kept telling him, "Are you going to talk trash about me and my family anymore?" Jose, struggling to get free, started cursing at Danny to put him down. My brother threw him into a snow bank. Jose got up and came at Danny again only this time Danny picked him up by the neck from behind and pressed the back of Jose's head into his tight arm, making it very difficult for Jose to breath. My brother whispered in Jose's ear that he had better stay away from him and his family or it was going to be worse the next time around for him. He then threw him into the snow bank again. By now my dad had arrived at the bus stop and saw Danny fighting with Jose. There was a car driving slowly in front of my dad, so he pulled over and started running down the street to break it up. My dad got to Danny as he threw Jose in the snow again. At that point

In Jamie's Words

my dad told Danny "Let's go. You proved your point." Jose ran home, crying hysterically, as my dad and brother walked to the car. My dad was upset that Danny got off of the bus at Jose's stop but was extremely proud that he stuck up for himself. When they got home, Danny told my mom what happened and she was very happy that he stuck up for his family and himself but was nervous that this wasn't over yet. A few minutes later Jose's dad was walking up our driveway, looking to start trouble with my dad. My dad stood on our front stoop and asked Jose Sr. what he wanted. He was rambling on about Danny getting dropped off at his house so that he could beat up his son. My dad calmly said "Is that what your son told you, because he's a liar and you should talk to him about what he's been saying and doing to my son." Jose Sr. left abruptly and my dad came inside. My mom still knew that this wasn't over yet.

Jose had a very dysfunctional home life. His mom and dad were divorced and he lived with his mom and her boyfriend. He used to live with his dad and go to another school but he must have caused too much trouble there so he now lived with his mother and

In Jamie's Words

as you can see was still causing lots of trouble in this school as well. Jose was the type of kid that hung out on the street late at night and damaged people's property, especially over a school break when there wasn't a curfew for him and he didn't have to worry about school. One night my parents saw him on the street corner at 1:00 am in the morning when they were on their way home from work at the catering hall that they were working at. Honestly, what is a 12 year old kid doing on a street corner at 1 am alone? Where is his mother? Don't parents realize that you have to be an important part of your child's life or nothing good will come out of it? Unlike Jose's parents, my parents were really hands on and took a personal interest in my siblings and my upbringing.

Christmas break was over and we had a great time off from school with my parents. We did so much together as a family. My parents spent a lot of time reminiscing about fun times when they met and fun places and activities that they did with my brother, sister and me when we were younger. My mom and dad would always tell us stories about how things were when they were kids.

In Jamie's Words

For example, there weren't any computers or cell phones so kids spent a lot of time doing activities together outside like playing kickball, handball, rollerblading, fishing, etc. When it came to getting along with other kids, if you had a fight with the schoolyard bully, it ended with that. No one chimed in afterwards or started a blog or put it on YouTube. Our society has changed so much. Why do we have to conform to the new ways? I understand that technology is different now but was it created to help our society or ruin it? Why did we have to become such targets for so long? Where were Amelia's parents and why weren't they as involved in her life like my parents were in ours? Did the situation with Amelia and her posse taint our lives forever? There were so many questions but no answers. The end result was that we wanted peace and we didn't know if we were ever going to get it.

It was January 4th, the holidays were over and it was time for my brother to go back to school. My brother had gotten over his confrontation with Jose and really wasn't worried about seeing him. My dad dropped him off at school. Danny didn't seem worried at all. He was too consumed with walking in with some of his friends to care about where Jose was. Second period rolled around and Danny saw his friend Stuart. Danny knew Stuart from elementary school and was looking forward to reconnecting with him when he got to middle school. Stuart pulled Danny aside and told him to watch his back because he was going to get **SHANKED!** Danny was confused and didn't understand what Stuart meant, so he said, "Stuart, what do you mean? Who's going to shank me?" Stuart said that Jose was really angry at him and that he had better watch his back. My brother had never heard the term "shank" so he really didn't know what it meant. I guess Danny wasn't up on his *"jail lingo"*. You see, Stuart's dad had been in jail for a long time so I guess he learned this from him. My brother finished out the rest of his classes and sent my dad a text at the end of the day telling him what Stuart told. My dad told him that the word shanked meant that he was going to get stabbed. My dad told him that he had to go to the principal and let her know what was said and what threat was made. Danny tried to go to the office but no one was there to listen.

In Jamie's Words

Danny got on the bus and was very worried now because Jose was on that bus. Danny kept his eye on him the whole bus ride until he got off the bus. Danny came running home and my mom immediately took him to Stuart's house to talk to him about the warning he gave Danny. They banged and banged on the door but Stuart refused to answer. You could see him peeking through the curtains looking at them but he never came. My mom and brother left and went to the district office where they spoke to the middle school superintendent. The superintendent said that he would do his best to get in touch with the principal to let her know the threat that was made and that we would be able to meet with the superintendent in about an hour because he wasn't in the building either.

Danny and my mom left the district more upset than when they got there. When they got back to the house my dad was there and he took him up to the middle school to speak to the principal but once again she wasn't available to speak to him. They got back in the car and drove to Stuart's house. When they got there his mom was home and she let them in. Stuart was pretending to sleep on the couch covered by a large blanket over his body and his face. My dad told Stuart's mom what happened and she asked my dad if she could speak to Stuart about it and then call us; my dad, of course, said yes. My dad and Danny came home very distraught. My mom took Danny back to school to meet with the superintendent. Finally, he gave my mom and brother a few minutes of his time. I guess since our tax dollars are paying him a hefty salary of $387,000 a year and his partner in crime, the assistant superintendent a salary of $200,000 a year, we were now eligible to speak with him for 15 minutes. My brother explained what happened and that we all tried to tell the principal what was going on but she was nowhere to be found. Even the superintendent tried and couldn't locate her. The superintendent took notes and said that he would get back to us in the morning. Well that was worth it…don't you think? You would have expected him to call Jose's parents and bring them right down but he didn't. I guess if his salary was $400,000 a year plus perks we would have gotten some satisfaction and Jose's parents would have received a phone call! There's nothing like using our hard earned tax

308

In Jamie's Words

dollars to fund bullying throughout the district. The school district

helping us was like a Three Toed Sloth having four toes!

The next day Danny went to school and Stuart stayed home.

What else did you expect? He was like a little weasel. Danny was

called down to the office and asked to explain what had happened.

Danny told them the story and then they called down Jose. Jose told

them that he didn't do anything and that he didn't know what they

were talking about. He also told the principal that it was Danny who

started a fight with him after they got off the bus on December 23rd

and that Danny was the one who should be punished. So what do

you think happened next? The principal called my mom and told

her that she was suspending my brother for 5 days out of school for

having a fight with Jose off school property because Danny got off

at Jose's bus stop with the intention of starting a fight. My mom told

her that she would be up in the morning to discuss the situation. The

next morning, my parents and Danny went to the middle school and

recorded the conversation of the principal and assistant principal

saying that Jose was afraid of Danny because of how big he was and

In Jamie's Words

that Jose never had a knife at all. Ms. Piper told my parents that she spoke with Jose's parents and they confirmed that he does have a knife but he didn't have it in school that day. My mom looked at them and said "And you believe them?" "Of course we do." They said. So my brother had to take the 5 days out of school suspension for doing nothing while he was threatened to be killed with a knife that the whole class knew about and the school wasn't willing to do anything about. My mom and dad went back to the superintendent's office who said that he was fully aware that Jose had a knife. I guess he was ok with the fact that this boy was allowed to carry a weapon to school. They decided to move my brother to another middle school and not punish Jose because they knew that he would strike again. Can you imagine the superintendent saying that he knew that Jose would strike again? We have all of this on tape as well and sometimes we just listen to it for the hell of it because it's so amusing!

CHAPTER FOURTEEN

FIGHTING BACK

We had finally had enough! I know you've heard us say this before but we were truly finished. We had been trapped like rats inside our home, not being able to sell it and having to endure years of abuse for no reason. Some of these kids don't even know why they were abusing us. They just felt like it because they wanted to be cool. But it wasn't just the kids. It was being victimized by the school district as well. How could the school in good conscience allow this to

In Jamie's Words

happen to us? We didn't do anything wrong, and yet we had been victimized for more than half of the years that we had lived in our home. The time had come to where I was going to prevail over this and take me and my family from Victim to Hero.

I remember my mom reading the newspaper and seeing that Legislator Jon Cooper was looking to pass a Suffolk County Cyber-Bullying Law. I asked my mom to please call him and see if we could meet with him to tell him our story. My mom agreed and called his office. They were extremely receptive and gave us an appointment right away. I was so excited; finally someone of authority was going to listen to what happened to me and my family after so many years of people not listening at all and shying away from us. We went to his office and showed him all of the evidence that we had against the school district. He was completely appalled. He couldn't believe that a school would allow this behavior to go on for so long and do nothing about it. He completely understood what happened to me, my brother and my parents as a result of this insanity.

In Jamie's Words

It wasn't long before my dad and I had our sleeves rolled up and we were diving in to help write the Cyber-Bullying Law. Before you knew it we had helped write the Suffolk County Law and we left with a mock up copy that just needed a few more revisions. I was so happy that my voice was heard and that I got to take part in the making of a law. Then I really started to think about what it would be like to go to school and have a safe and educational environment without bullies. Can you imagine not being afraid to go to school? How many teens do you think are afraid to go to school every day because of bullying? The answer is approximately 200,000 teens stay home across the country everyday because of bullying. Wow, I needed to do more research to see what other bullying statistics I could find out. This would help me to shed my skin and become empowered so that I could help others. Then I realized that it's one thing to be bullied by your peers and another to be bullied by the faculty, principal and superintendent. We needed a law in place that would prevent this from happening to anyone ever again. I wrote my thoughts down and decided to make another appointment with Legislator Jon Cooper to discuss what I called "The School Accountability Law" otherwise known as "Jamie's Law." I designed it to be a 3 strike system, where, if you've been bullied and you tell the principal and nothing is done to stop it and it continues and you tell them again and again and still nothing is done to apprehend the bully, then the principal is punished with a fine and misdemeanor. I had big hopes for this law because I knew that if there was a law like this in place, then all of the bullying that my brother and I endured would have ended very quickly and would never have gone this far!

Knowing that my mom had taken a year off from work just so she could go to the library to brush up on her state educational laws really got me thinking. I started to think that it was my turn now to read some of those laws and know them myself. So, that's exactly what I did. I needed to be able to speak before the Suffolk County Legislature if I wanted this Cyber-Bullying Law to pass as well as The School Accountability Law/Jamie's Law. I did a lot of research as well as writing my speeches to include a little bit about my bullied past and my plans to stand up and make a change. That day finally came and I got a chance to speak to a whole room of Suffolk County Legislators and read them my speech that I had diligently prepared. They only give you 5 minutes to speak so you really have to make sure that you say all of the important things that you need to say before your time is up. I would practice my speech over and over while my dad timed me; there was no way I was going to walk away from that podium without saying everything that needed to be said.

Even though this amazing thing was happening I was still carrying such a heavy heart for my brother because he was still having so many problems with Jose and his friends due to the knife incident. My dad spoke to the legislators regarding all of the incidents surrounding my brother's case in between the break for lunch and they were all very taken back by the continued abuse. Legislator John Kennedy made a phone call over to the precinct and spoke to the Deputy Inspector who wanted to see us right away. We immediately went across to his building and met with him and the

Lieutenant. They sat with us for about an hour and said that they would put a team on it and go to each bully's house to warn them to stay away from us, as well as speak to their parents to make them aware of what their kids were doing. Well, this is exactly what we had in mind...an arrest was what we really wanted but we weren't going to turn down a warning to each kid. So, we carried out our plan to make a change not only for me and my brother, but for kids all over the world who were afraid to go to school. I was determined to be the voice of all the bullied victims who had no voice or who had taken their lives because they couldn't get out from under the sadness. I was on an unstoppable mission and each and every day I was becoming more confident and empowered!

One morning we actually woke up to news trucks outside our home. We couldn't believe it. My mom hopped in the shower so fast while my dad threw clothes on and ran outside to ask them if they could give us about an hour to get ready. My mom couldn't believe this was happening. She kept saying, "I can't believe after all of these years and all of the torment, we are actually going to be

In Jamie's Words

heard." One by one, the camera crews came in our home. At one point, while my mom and dad were being interviewed, I was asked to give an interview for a radio station. It was complete chaos, but in a good way. One of the news networks asked if we would mind taking a ride to the elementary school where it had all began; of course we agreed. The interview was amazing. The entire faculty watched through the windows as I walked down the sidewalk with a news reporter telling my story and pointing at the school. At one point, security showed up and just watched. There was nothing anyone could do; we hadn't stepped a foot on their property. We were just walking back and forth on the sidewalk in front of the school just to annoy them. If you looked closely you could see the infamous principal peering through the shade that she had pulled down. It was like a scene in a creepy horror movie, when they peek through a crack. Whatever it was, it was all good and I felt extremely empowered that day and I felt like I had gotten one up on the principal and the school.

Afterwards we returned home. I was so excited; it was like someone had left a light on in my head and I was thinking of so many things I could do to make a change. My mind was racing as I wrote down some ideas that I thought would work in changing the way kids felt about their peers. Then, it came to me...I told my parents that I wanted to form a foundation that would incorporate all of the tactics that we used to keep me safe and alive as well as including all of the people we had in our immediate circle that played a key role. My parents were so excited with this idea. They couldn't believe that we hadn't thought of this before. I wasn't surprised though because we were so engrossed in the day to day bullying that we couldn't see the light. I almost felt like I handed my parents a shovel to dig themselves out; that's truly what this idea felt like.

My parents immediately got started on incorporating our non-profit and we decided to call it "The Jamie Isaacs Foundation For Anti-Bullying Inc." We were all working so hard to put it together in time for the next legislature meeting for the Suffolk

In Jamie's Words

County Cyber-Bullying Law because I wanted to be able to announce it to all of the legislators who had taken an interest in me. We worked diligently ordering the purple silicone bracelets that say "Put a Stop to Bullying" with the foundation logo on the inside and all of our printed material that needed our logo. We hired this amazing computer web designer who created our website www.jamieisaacsfoundation.org in a very short period of time. It was all coming together like it was meant to be.

It was time for the next legislature meeting and I was fully prepared! Once again when we arrived the media greeted us. They were swarming us asking if the Cyber-Bullying Law would pass along with my Accountability Law. I told them that I was hoping for the best. Inside we noticed that principals and superintendents came from all over New York State to fight The School Accountability Law/Jamie's Law. They all turned to look at me when I walked in to find a seat. One at a time they were called up to give their 5 minute speech on why they thought my bill shouldn't pass. We sat for so long just listening to all of them tell the legislators that it was the

In Jamie's Words

parent's responsibility, not theirs, to raise the students properly. My dad and I couldn't wait until it was our turn to say what we had experienced for so long with the school district. About 2 hours had gone by and finally it was my turn. I stood at the podium with such confidence and told the legislators that students like me who are bullied desperately need a law like this to be passed to protect them and that if there was a law in place like this one than what happened to me and my brother would have never happened. When my 5 minutes were up, one of the legislators applauded me and said loudly, *"Jamie, you've turned lemons into lemonade."* With that they all applauded me, except the principals and superintendents that came to nix the bill. Then my dad got called to go up and speak and his speech was amazing! He gave a parent's perspective on what it was like to have such turmoil take over a home and lives as a result of a schools negligence. My dad was also commended on his speech. When it was time to speak about the Cyber-Bullying Law, I spoke from the heart and proudly supported the bill and told the legislators that a bill like this must pass to stop the suicides.

In Jamie's Words

Afterwards, we felt relieved that we had gone and done such a great thing, even though so many came out to speak out against it. I wasn't annoyed at all that these principals and superintendents came out to speak against my bill. Even the school psychologist from the middle school that I transferred out of came out to defend the school but it didn't matter. What mattered was that I was the reason they all came out to veto the bill. Can you image; first my voice isn't heard for over 6 years and now there's a room filled with principals and superintendents who had gone out of their way to fight against what I had to say? Wow, if that's not empowering I don't know what is.

This was the reason I was thrust into the spotlight. It wasn't all of the bullying I endured or that my family endured: it was the fact that now I was pointing a finger at an authority figure. So did it really matter if the School Accountability Law passed or not? It definitely got the stir we were looking for and as a result kids came out of the woodwork to tell their stories to the news as well. I guess they figured if Jamie Isaacs can do it so can they. Needless to say

In Jamie's Words

'The School Accountability Law" did not pass. It was reduced down to a task force and then withdrawn. At first I was sad but then I realized that it was withdrawn because "The Dignity for All Students Act" was passed on a State Level and must be in effect for the year 2012. I was still in the spotlight and we had just received confirmation that The Suffolk County Cyber-bullying Law had just passed!

CHAPTER FIFTEEN

SAVING LIVES

We designed our brochures, completed the website, had our first board meeting and launched our 24 hour hotline. I never felt so alive! I started to think about all of the teens that had taken their lives and realized that they were never able to feel what I was feeling at that very moment. They would never feel victory or glory. All they felt was unbelievable sadness that they let get the best of them forever. At that very moment, I vowed that I would do anything in my power to make teens realize their self worth and that even though they had a bad day or a bad week or month, things would get better if they just believed in themselves.

My dad put a call into People Magazine and left them a detailed message about what I had accomplished with regard to being bullied for over 6 consecutive years and then helping to write and pass the Suffolk County Cyber-Bullying Law. Monica, one of the executives from People, contacted us right away and told my mom that she knew exactly who I was and she wanted all of my information in the form of a bio sent to her for review. Shortly after that we received a phone call from one of their senior reporters to do an interview. The reporter interviewed my mom only to get the basic idea of what took place with the bullies and me and then spoke to me for approximately 2 hours to get the whole story. The reporter wasn't sure when the article was being printed but told us that we would be receiving a phone call as to when it would be. My mom had many conversations with Monica after that and then finally it came to fruition; Monica called and asked my mom to bring me into

In Jamie's Words

Manhattan that week for my photo shoot. We received a phone call from the head photographer to schedule the exact date of it. I couldn't believe it...I was going to be featured in People Magazine! It was an incredible honor and an amazing feeling to get justice in the form of world recognition for fighting back and not allowing the bullies to take away myself worth and my life. I was extremely proud.

My mom and I took the train into Manhattan with this huge garment bag filled with several changes of clothes; we wanted to make sure we made the right outfit choice. When we arrived at the studio there was a huge buffet set up for us like we were celebrities or something. Just knowing that celebrities had been photographed in that studio with a similar spread of food was so empowering for me, I was beaming! The photographers were ready for me; they had adjusted the lighting and the back drop to conform to my clothing color and instantly started taking pictures. They literally took hundreds of shots. I was so excited I wanted to scream but I had to compose myself and scream within. Afterwards, they let us look at the photos. They were unbelievable. The colors were so rich and vibrant not like any pictures I've ever seen. I asked which one they were going to choose and they showed us a few of the choices. My mom asked if they knew when the issue was going to available in the stores and they weren't sure; they said it could be right away or within the month. Well, within 10 days the magazine was on the shelves in every store all over the world! I was part of the cover story of the October 18th, 2010 issue called "Deadly Bullying." My story was featured on page 69 along with my photo. I received several Facebook requests from kids all over the world that said that they read my story and they wanted to speak to me about their bullying situation. I couldn't believe it, how did these kids find me so quickly? There was one teen in particular from Ohio that I developed a great relationship with. She really wasn't being bullied but was inspired by what I've done to save myself and make a change. She wanted to know how she could help in Ohio to make changes there as well. We had spoken several times and I gave her some really good ideas about how to make huge changes in small

In Jamie's Words

steps. I couldn't believe it, now kids were looking to me for advice? If someone would have told me that this was going to happen to me after so many years of abuse, I would have said "NO WAY!" Maybe that legislator was right, maybe I did turn lemons into lemonade?

It was November and we scheduled our first fundraiser at a local bowling alley. We hired an event planner who organized the whole thing. So many people showed up to support us including most of the faculty from The Knox School where I currently attend. We had many kids show up who were being bullied from schools all over Long Island. They wanted to meet me and have my foundation help them. I had been interviewed by WBLI 106.1 a local Long Island radio station that helped spread the word for me prior to the fundraiser, so they came down to show their support. It was such a magical day; we gave out our purple silicon "Put a Stop to Bullying" bracelets along with t-shirts to everyone that came down. Legislator John Kennedy came to award me with a Proclamation for my continued good deeds in the community. We raised enough money to get started so that we could really help other teens in crisis.

328

In Jamie's Words

The phone calls had started to come in; between the local newspaper articles for the passing of the Cyber-Bullying Law, the People Magazine article and now the radio station interview, it wasn't long before the word was out that there might be help for bullied victims. One of the first victims we helped was a 14 year old from Nassau County who came to my fundraiser because we had reached out to him and his family after reading his story in a local newspaper. Our child advocate called several meetings with the principal and superintendent of the boy's school until he was able to get his problem resolved. For starters, we were able to change his schedule so that the first 3 classes were bully free and then a private school bus picked him up and took him to the local library to be homeschooled for the rest of his classes. Then he was returned to school to participate in his sport at the end of the day. This went on for months until he felt safe and secure about returning to school fulltime. The parents were so grateful to us, especially his mom who was so beside herself from all of the continued abuse. Sometimes I would hear my mom on the phone with his mom late at night talking to her about staying positive even though it felt nearly impossible.

This whole experience was so amazing for all of us. My mom couldn't believe how good she felt after speaking with some of the victims and their families; my mom realized that all these years when she felt so alone and isolated there were so many others in the same position. Yet when it's happening you feel like you're the only one. My mom embraced what was happening with open arms and truly understood that her purpose in life had just changed and that it now was to make a difference in people's lives and do God's work to save lives and create peace. This newfound purpose was fine with my mom, especially since her wounds were still open and healing; by helping others it helped her to heal as well. My dad was on another mission; he became an Ordained Interfaith Minister. He had thought about this for a long time and decided that he needed to heal within and before he could help others he needed to help himself and by doing so and understanding other people's faiths, he would better understand how to help them. It took my dad a few months of taking courses online, studying and reading the Bible to pass various tests, and become Reverend Doctor Ronald Isaacs. It was truly a remarkable thing that my dad did. How many Jewish men read the Bible and become an ordained minister? This showed me more so than ever that my family pulled together to make the unbelievable happen. My parents had so much love for each other and they never lost that glow; maybe behind closed doors they argued over the persistent bullying and harassment that had encompassed our lives but we were all on the same page now and it was truly inspirational.

Soon, the calls for help were coming in nonstop. One parent called to tell us that their child was assaulted by a security guard at school and nothing was done. In this case we put them in touch with our attorney, Mitch Carlinsky. Another parent called to tell us that their teen had been suicidal due to all of the abuse and they didn't want to hospitalize her but didn't know what to do to keep her safe. After many conversations with the child and her parents, we chose to keep them in touch with our social worker. She is an intricate part of The Jamie Isaacs Foundation and helps to keep victims and their families on the right track mentally. Another parent contacted us and told us that her daughter wasn't going to take it anymore and she was going to continue retaliating until she got it to stop, even if it meant that she got suspended or expelled. My mom had many long conversations with this mother. You see, it's one thing to stand up for yourself and it's another to retaliate just because someone looks at you the wrong way. Some kids just need the right tactics to understand people. You can't go through your whole life being angry at the world and viewing life with such animosity. You need to learn that there are certain situations that require you to defend yourself physically and other situations that require you to back off and let it go while other situations need the assistance of an adult or someone of authority. Because of our long journey we are able to offer the right advice to families in crisis. The team that we carefully put together consisting of my parents, the social worker, child advocate, attorney and of course myself, the victim, is able to give extraordinary advice and give a point of view that sometimes isn't seen because of all of the surrounding turmoil. In this situation we called many meetings with the principal and placed this child on home schooling until she felt confident enough to go back to school without hurting anyone. You see, if you repeatedly retaliate when it comes time to get the bully in trouble it won't work out to your benefit because you will be viewed as the bully as well and how many suspensions do you want on your record?

I would have to say that one of the most rewarding calls we received was from a parent who was living in a shelter with 3 young boys ages 11, 9 and 3. Her husband had been in prison. She lost her home and was forced to take herself and her children to a shelter. My mom had never encountered an experience like this, but when the call came in she knew that something had to be done immediately. The woman told my mom her children were having problems with other kids in the shelter and that no one was willing to help. They were all fending for themselves, even if it meant that they had to steal from each other to fulfill their needs. The oldest boy was being harassed in school with kids telling him that he was "homeless" and therefore "worthless." This case truly broke my mother's heart and my mom took it personally. My mom met with this woman in a different location than the shelter and discussed a plan. My mother knew so many contacts from agencies all over New York State, so she called them to see if anyone could move this family out.

It seemed as though there was no hope due to Section 8 housing being closed. This didn't stop my mom from investing months into helping this woman. During this time, our foundation put together a support group program for the summer and invited the oldest son to attend along with many other teens. Not only was this an amazing opportunity to connect with bullied victims on a more personal level, but we were able to see such change in these teens; their whole demeanors had changed and they became more positive about themselves as the weeks went on. My brother even attended the support groups and found peace within. The great thing was that my mom got to connect with this woman before each support group to discuss any progress in moving them out. Even though this woman wasn't attending the support group because of privacy acts between the kids, we noticed her attitude changing as well for the positive. It was almost as if she had a reason to live now. She would tell my mom how hard it was for her doing this alone with the kids and how grateful she was that we were there to help. One day, my mom had an idea that she was going to start calling brokers who were looking to rent an apartment or home out and discussed the possibility of renting it to someone who was currently living in a shelter and on public assistance. Well, it must have been *fate* because one broker asked to meet my mom to discuss this further and as it turned out she was able to rent this woman and her 3 children an apartment right away! This woman recently called the hotline to tell my mom that "she is the reason that her and her 3 kids are alive and that without my mom there was no reason to go on." She told my mom that "she will be forever grateful for the undying attempts that she made unconditionally without even knowing her and her children before." This woman was crying so hard that she couldn't catch her breath, which of course made my mother cry hysterically with her. My mom told her that the pleasure was all hers, and that if she could do it again she would. You see…this is what it's all about!

One of the most interesting phone calls we received was from CPS (Child Protective Services). This phone call was extremely rewarding to say the least. The gentleman that my mom spoke was given a case where the child was bullied in school and therefore had ongoing problems there. The school that called CPS probably should have just done their job and fixed the problem themselves, but that's what's wrong with these districts. They're all from the same mold and mentality…if there's a problem and you can't fix it, just call CPS on the family and they'll fix it. Or, if the school can't fix it, because they refuse to try to… just call an ambulance and have the kid taken away and put in a mental institution and ruin the child's credibility for the rest of his or her life! You can't believe how many phone calls like this we have received. As far as the CPS case went, we called a hearing and were able to place the child in another school within the same school district and everything was fine after that. Now why couldn't the principal just work this out with the superintendent and the parents and come to a comfortable decision together? Why did they have to involve CPS? It really should be a crime to allow school districts to make these life changing calls to these government agencies that can potentially take your child away from you if they see fit, when the whole time it could be resolved between the parents and the school.

I find it interesting when people call the hotline whether it is the victim or their parents, their incidents may be different, but the end result is always the same. The school district is always at fault for not protecting the student. So far, we haven't come across a case where the principal or superintendent fixed a problem to the fullest and reprimanded the bully and resolved the problem completely for the victim. It's sad, don't you think, to work so hard to pay your taxes... then to have so many problems with the principal and superintendent, the very people that *your* hard earned tax dollars pay.

Even though I'm only 15 years old, I'm way beyond my years because of everything that has happened to me and my family.

In Jamie's Words

Some people may view this as being a bad thing because I am so mature for my age, but I view it as a blessing. God opened my eyes to a world that needs help and there are not enough people to help, so I'm glad that I have been chosen to go on this journey to help others to see the light. I can honestly say that I love what I do and I would not have wanted it any other way. I have done so many in school presentations all over Long Island and when these kids see me, they are fascinated. It's like I'm a celebrity. I walk in and they give me a standing ovation. It gives me the chills when they respond to me in that fashion when most of my childhood years were plagued with torment and grief and now I'm their hero!

I have truly been taken back by the response that I get at a school or camp presentation. After it's over, kids come up to me and ask if they can speak with me privately about their bullying problem; of course I say yes. They have all confided in me and told me that they have attempted suicide multiple times and they want to be strong like me. They have all asked if they can stay in touch with me in the event that feeling comes over them again so that they have me to talk them out of it. Usually at this point I tell them to call the foundation in the event they have the urge to hurt themselves because it's a huge responsibility for me in the event that they go through with their suicide plan. Otherwise I'm always willing to talk to them and help them through any bullying problem that they might have and helping them stay positive. There have been lots of times that I have told kids to contact me through my Facebook fan page so they feel as though they are not alone, and there have been many times that victims have reached out to me. It's a wonderful feeling knowing that I'm important to so many young teens out there that have so many questions and problems but no answers.

The best part of helping people for me and my family is when we have successfully given the victim a bully free day at school or we have moved them to another school within the district to begin their new life. The "Thank You" letters and emails that we have received truly make it all worthwhile. Some parents have told my mom that "she's an Angel sent from Heaven" while others have said "if it wasn't for us they would have lost their child to suicide."

In Jamie's Words

These families are ***desperate*** for help…just like we were. The only difference is that we are here to help them; when it was happening to us we were left to figure things out on our own until we made these unbelievable contacts and connections with all of the right people that have now enabled us to successfully fix the bullying problem.

CHAPTER SIXTEEN

JUSTICE SERVED

The journey has been so long for my family and me, but we never gave up. There were so many times that I wanted to throw in the towel and never did. I would see the disgust on my parents' faces when they felt as though their wheels were just spinning and nothing was getting done, but I knew that there were so many more victims that needed to be saved and more awareness that needed to be created, so I wasn't giving up so quickly. Sometimes I would sit

In Jamie's Words

in front of my computer and scroll through all the stories about teen suicides and I would get so angry that it was because of other teens that they ended their lives. I understand the reason behind the pain that they were feeling, for at that very moment they were in such a dark, lonely place but eventually that pain would have passed and they would have seen the light. Someone once told me that it's hard to see the sun through the clouds, but that does not mean that it's not there. How do you know what life has in store for you if you're willing to let someone take your dreams and hopes away? I wasn't ready to have my bright future taken away by some jealous, envious bully that wished she were me or wished she had my life. I'm proud of who I am and I believe in myself enough not to believe the hurtful things that people say. I knew that if I kept making appearances in schools and the media continued to cover my progress with passing laws, bullying would remain in the forefront and it would also give other teens the window of opportunity to come forward with their bullying stories.

In Jamie's Words

One day, my mom received a phone call from Beverly Fortune, the Associate Publisher of The Long Island Press, telling her that I was nominated as a "Woman of Distinction." I could not believe that I would receive such an award just for fighting back and coming forward with my story and trying to make a change in the community. I didn't take a stand so that I could receive an award; I did it to stop the suicides; I did it because no one else was doing it and it needed to be done. I could not believe that I was being nominated, along with other women much older than me, for this amazing achievement. I was so nervous that night when Beverly told my story to hundreds of people that came to the event. She started to cry when she spoke about all of the torment that I endured, and after a few moments I realized that she was talking about me. You see, I had been through so much that it was almost as if I erased it from my mind even though I kept it in my heart. When I heard her talk about my journey I looked at my mom who was standing near the stage that I was on and she was crying. At that moment I realized that I did do something heroic…I didn't take my life! At the end of the ceremony I was given a Certificate of Recognition from a representative from New York State Governor Andrew Cuomo's office who made it a point to get on stage and tell the audience what an amazing young woman I am and how proud she was of me. The evening was magical and so many people attending came over to congratulate me. My family and I were so proud that we were included in such a magnificent event and that I was recognized in this fashion. I truly felt unstoppable after that evening, almost as if I had no boundaries or limits. I told my mom to continue on her path in getting me recognition because I finally felt as though we had found our purpose in life. Sometimes it takes something like this to make you realize that the road you were on is the wrong one, that you need to open your eyes and see what you were put on this earth to accomplish.

Soon afterwards, my mom was able to get me into the April/May Issue '11 of Girls Life Magazine. They were doing an article on looking at the brighter side of life and what teens can do to make it through. I was lucky enough to have a portion of my story

In Jamie's Words

incorporated in the article; this was a very exciting moment for me to be part of such a heavily read teen magazine. Then I thought I would do something really cool and talk to the salon where I get my hair done and ask if they would consider holding a promotion to help raise money for my foundation by doing purple hair extensions. We did it for the month of May and it went over really great. I even got it approved by the Knox School to have the hair extensions done there for one day. It was a great idea that helped my foundation continue the awareness.

My mom received an email from the Governor's office saying that the he was going to be appearing at a local college to speak about some of his proposed bills and I was invited to attend. My parents and I went to his press conference and at the end I was able to meet and shake hands with the Governor. It was a great experience for me and my parents. Soon after that, the same office representative sent my mom an email the morning of Memorial Day, asking if I would walk in the parade with the Governor; I could not believe it. I was going to walk with the Governor of New York in the Memorial Day Parade! I quickly got ready and my dad brought me to the location of the parade where I was greeted by the Governor's security (Secret Service) and escorted over to his vehicle were the Governor happily acknowledged me. This moment will be with me forever.

Over the summer, I was asked to take part in a Documentary about bullying. I felt that this would be a fantastic opportunity to be interviewed and tell the world what my family and I had been through for so many years. My parents were interviewed as well to give a "parents perspective" into the effects that bullying can have on the whole family, not just the victim. It was difficult for my parents to be interviewed because they were still very emotionally connected to what happened to us as a result of the bullying and the long term effects that it had on our family. For me, this was a very exciting moment more so than anything that I had ever done because the director truly wanted to know how it felt to be bullied. Even though other teens were interviewed in this Documentary, it was an amazing experience to have been chosen to partake in such an amazingly well put together film portraying what it is really like to be bullied. I was happy that I was able to portray what it was like for me to be a victim for over 6 years and then watch it happen to my brother by the same kids. I hope that when the Documentary called *"Bullycide: The Voice of Complicity"* is released, it is as compelling as the real truth behind bullying and all of its effects.

The summer was very busy for me in general, not just with the Documentary but with many other appearances and gatherings. I was asked to participate in The AllyKatz Year of the Youth Culmination held at the United Nations Building in New York City. This was an unbelievable experience all around because I was nominated to be a youth delegate. I was able to attend seminars and ask questions and voice my opinion to other teens who were chosen as well. I spoke with magazine editors and posed with some amazing stars for photos. The day was truly inspirational! It's days like this that I would have missed out on if I would have let the bullies get the best of me!

In Jamie's Words

I was also asked to become part of the Congress for Justice/Suffolk County Youth Bureau located in Suffolk County, New York. Accepting this opportunity meant a lot of dedication and time on my part. The students that make up the Congress of Justice are from schools across Suffolk County and are of the same mentality as me. These teens care about themselves, have a positive outlook on life and are no longer intimidated by the bullies. It's one thing to get bullied, but it's another to let it bother you and eat away at you until you're stripped of your dignity and self worth. The Congress of Justice has so many core values that it's important to understand what they stand for ...to carry out *"Justice"* within our schools and our community. One of the main things that I enjoy doing with The Congress of justice is setting up "Justice Clubs" in schools so that kids feel as though they have the support from their peers to turn to if they're being bullied. The purpose of this club is to almost act as a *"task force"* to control bullying and diffuse it as a team as soon as it occurs. Originally I was asked to be their Keynote Speaker at their anti-bullying summit, but then they saw how dedicated I was and how willing I was to help out continuously as opposed to just at the summit. I feel that this is one of the most important commitments I have ever made.

In life you have to remember that every day counts and to make sure that you make the best of it because you don't know what tomorrow will bring. I try to find time every day to do something kind or show someone who I barely know support in some way. I have found that there are so many people out there that are just existing, not living...kind of what was happening to me and my family when all of the bullying started. I will never let life pass me by anymore and I think that I speak for my family as well. Try to make the most of every day and if you can help someone or make a change along the way then you have done something great! With this being said, I willingly accepted the task that was put before me when my mom received a phone call from State Senator Jeffrey Klein's office. Apparently, Senator Klein, from the Bronx, was doing research, along with Senator Savino and Senator Carlucci, on bullying/cyber-bullying and came across my foundation and all of my accomplishments and decided to have one of his staff reach out to us. I must say that this was truly an amazing, life changing call. My mom accepted the opportunity that was put forth before her to have me assist in the passing of the New York State Cyber-Bullying Law that would now hold the perpetrator on second degree manslaughter charges if convicted in a cyber-bullying incident that resulted in the victim taking his or her own life. We were asked to join Senator Klein, Senator Savino and Senator Carlucci at a press conference in Manhattan in front of the Criminal Court Building. I couldn't wait to meet the Senators and take part in such a monumental moment, when Senator Klein would reveal his plans to make such an enormous change in our society today. The new Cyber-Bullying Law will become an extension of the New York State "Stalking Law", which currently does not include Cyber-Bullying. This bill would make online bullying of a minor considered **Third Degree Stalking** which is a Class A Misdemeanor…and those responsible for a suicide due to Cyber-Bullying would be charged with **Second Degree Manslaughter**

In Jamie's Words

which is a Class C Felony punishable by up to 15 years in prison. I could not believe that I would now become part of the passing of this incredible bill. As I participated in the press conference, I was overcome by such emotion for at that moment I realized that I too was changing the world and making history.

I was then asked to appear on NY1 "Inside City Hall" talk show along with Senator Klein. I was so proud, just the thought of being on a talk show that politicians are on blew me away! I happened to be in Manhattan that day with my Creative Writing Class seeing an Off Broadway Show when my mom pulled up in a hired car that the talk show sent for me to take me to their studio. Once I got there the rush was on. I had only minutes to get changed out of my school uniform and transform myself to be on TV. My mom watched from a separate room as me and the Senator where filmed. It was so exciting...I loved every minute of it. That evening it aired and I received messages through my website from strangers telling me what a strong person I am and that what I'm doing is inspiring. All I have to say is that I'm doing it because I want to, because I truly care.

In the midst of all of this I was also asked to take part in Non-Violence Month in Freeport, New York kick off on October 1st and 2nd with Mayor Andrew Hardwick. I was honored to participate in such an extraordinary weekend with the Mayor and his wonderful staff. They had so much planned for me. For starters, I was asked to speak at a church in Freeport where the event started off. It was so nice to sit and listen to other members from the Freeport community speak about continuing to spread peace throughout the neighborhood. Then, I was called up to speak; I was so eager to share my story, which I consider a journey to find peace. As I spoke I could see the expressions on their faces change as they listened to the torment that I endured. I guess from all of the times I shared my journey with people, I was truly able to heal. Honestly, I think that it made me so strong mentally that I'm now able to share my story in a way that it teaches teens to stand up for themselves and not let it destroy them. I think that the inner strength that I have found is the only reason I am able to make a change in the world for the better. I think that if I was still caught up in all of the drama, my presentations would not go over as well as they do because I'm now able to connect with every teen in the group whether they are the victim or the bully! Afterwards Mayor Hardwick honored me with a Citation.

October 2nd was just as great as the 1st. I was asked to speak at the Freeport Library for a two hour "Teacher Accredited" presentation. Teachers came from all over Nassau County to earn credits by listening to my Anti-Bulling Presentation. It's hard to believe isn't it, that a 15 year old would have the capability to give teachers educational credits? Some teachers brought their children while others came alone and couldn't wait for the presentation to start to see what it was really all about. As usual, I start with a little history about my bullying situation and then I talk about statistics, which then leads me to ask questions to the audience. I must say that this presentation went extremely well. It ran longer that 2 hours and people didn't want to leave because they were still absorbing what was said and what they could do to make a change as well. The day was amazing; once again I felt as though I had done something so needed in our society which was to share my experiences so others may benefit and learn from what I have been through and what I was able to overcome and accomplish.

Senator Jeff Klein asked me to participate in another press conference to be held in Queens. I was honored to be invited to take part in this press conference as well because I helped the Senator put together a census that he wanted to do throughout New York State to give him a better idea of the exact percentage of Cyber-Bullying victims. The Senator was going to discuss the census at the press conference and I was going to be the one who submitted the first one in front of all the media. What I didn't know was that I was about to meet Miss New York Kaitlin Monte. As soon as we were introduced we hit it off. She was so beautiful and stood for so many honorable things. Afterwards we exchanged information so that we can keep each other in the loop. I was very grateful to Senator Klein for this awesome experience and for making me such a significant part of his Cyber-Bullying Bill.

My family and I had many conversations with the Senator, but one of the most valuable ones was when he told me that he would like to appoint me to start up and run the New York State Youth Advisory Coalition which would be a group of students that would advise the Senate on the issues of bullying. I have to say that I didn't see this one coming. Of course I would jump at the chance to run such an organization that would advise the Senate of bullying issues across New York State. Who knew that my life was going to take a turn like this just because I stood up and fought for what I believed in?

Through it all the media followed me on my journey. News 12 just did an outstanding job on a special they had for the October 2011 show called "Making A Difference" which spotlighted me. I was honored that News 12 spent the day filming me at my home and then at school. It was a very special day for me because for so long I had yearned for this attention to tell my story and now I am the story of *Hope*!

I am blessed to have survived this unbelievable journey that had so many twists and turns. If it weren't for my faith and my family, my journey would have ended long ago, but with my parents undying love and support I was able to make it through, not only for me but for all of the bullied victims out there that needed me to make it through as well so that I may save them. If I had to choose to re-do my 15 years of life and have them be bully-free, I would probably choose to have my life go down the same road it has gone for I was chosen to do a job and help victims stand up and fight for what is right. I hope that all of the bullied victims and their families will support me now and in the future, as I prepare to speak before the New York State Senate in Albany NY to pass this extraordinary Cyber-Bullying Law that will make history and hopefully put an end to the horrible epidemic we call Bullying!

WORDS OF WISDOM

No matter what life throws at you, it's always important to stay strong and think positive. Always remember that it's just a bad day, not a bad life and you have the power to work through it. Suicide is not the answer and it never will be. If you just look on the bright side of everything you will be able to make it through the day knowing that tomorrow is a new day. Don't close doors, open them; opened doors allow for great opportunities for new friendships and that's something you should never let pass you by. I believe that in life there are no coincidences. It all happens because of fate. You might not think that fate plays a role when you're in a dark and lonely place; sometimes life gives us tests and we need to put our best effort forward. We can't be afraid to back down, run or hide when life puts us on a different path.

Life is a precious gift that no one should have taken away, especially by someone who is out to destroy you with harsh words, jealousy, envy and lies.

In Jamie's Words

EPILOGUE

You never know where life will take you. Sometimes you start off with certain goals and ambitions in life but for some reason you never fulfill them and wind up doing something you never dreamed of. Don't be afraid to take chances in life and accept was happens gracefully. Things might not always turn out the way you want them to, but in the end it can put you on a path that you never expected but still appreciate. Learn to appreciate every day and enjoy your friends and family to the fullest. Don't ever wish your

In Jamie's Words

life away or look to end it abruptly, for you will wish that you had a

second chance to make a change.

MY "PEACE" OF MIND

If it weren't for everything that happened to me, I would not be the strong person I am today. I am lucky to have had the support of my loving family who helped guide me through the toughest years of my life. I was tired of hearing that the fence needed to be mended, when the fence had already been torn down, or that I should just toughen up. I was tired of hearing that the faculty's hands were tied and they could not help me. I just wanted someone other than my family to show me they cared or that they were listening...and no one did until many years had passed. I was an innocent child who needed the help of an adult while in the care and supervision of the school district, who allowed me to slip through the cracks. I thought that I could count on the school psychologist, the school principal and assistant principal but to no avail, they all let me down. It was moments like this that I began to question what type of people the world is really made up of and how they could all turn a blind eye to what was going on right under their noses. How they could look me in the face and tell me that the bullies did nothing wrong? Or that it never happened. I'm not sure why these individuals chose to behave in this fashion, but for what it's worth, I had an inner strength that kept me alive and gave me the will to keep going.

The sad part is that all of the bullies continued to waste their precious time on harassing me, when they could have been doing so many things to better themselves. It's sad to think that they thought of different ways every day to torment me, as opposed to thinking of ways that they could have become better people, students and friends. Just to think…they must have felt so small because they all had to stay together in a click, since they were all too weak to act alone.

As for the parents of the bullies, they too needed to accept responsibility for what their children did, but they weren't willing to do that either. You see, the first step is admitting to the problem, the second step is fixing it, not pushing it under the carpet or pretending that it didn't happen. By not admitting what your child did, you did your child an injustice. This is truly the only way our society will ever get fixed. People have to be ready to admit their faults and shortcomings in order to make it right, but not everyone is willing to do that and until this happens, our society will continue to remain broken.

I am urging all of you to please take a stand in helping to make the world a safe place for our children. They are our future. I need more people join me in my fight to end **Hate** and **Violence** and spread *Kindness.*

In Jamie's Words

I thank each and every one of you that created and continued my torment for it opened my eyes to what was really going on in the world, for it is you that has to live with yourself.

Jamie presented with
an Award for
"Women of Distinction"
at the LI Press'
Fortune 52 event May 2011

NYS Senator David Carlucci, NYS Senator Diane
Savino, Jamie Isaacs and NYS Senator Jeffrey Klein

NY Cyberbully Press Conference
September 2011

New York State Senator
Jeffrey Klein with Jamie Isaacs

Jamie with Monique Coleman
from Disney's "High School Musical" at
Allykatz Year of the Youth Culmination August 2011

The Isaacs Family 2011 shown above: (L to R)
Danny, Ron, Jamie, Anne & Lindsey

Caroline Sunshine from Disney's "Shake it Up" with Jamie
at AllyKatz Year of the Youth Culmination August 2011

(Top) Suffolk County Legislator John M. Kennedy, Jr. With Ron, Jamie, Anne, Danny and Lindsey Isaacs & Grandma Vita Ciaramella

(Right) Duncan Marshall (Assistant Headmaster at Knox School), Beverly Fortune and Jamie & Anne Isaacs at LI Press' Fortune 52 event May 2011

(Below) Jamie & Anne Isaacs with the "Playground Peacemakers" Clara H. Carlson Elementary School In Elmont NY

Jamie is part of the Equestrian Team at the Knox School.

She has been riding since she was 7 years old.

Jamie is a Walk, Trot, Canter, Beginner, Jumper Equestrian.